In My Dreams

By
James T. Durkin

authorHOUSE™

1663 LIBERTY DRIVE, SUITE 200
BLOOMINGTON, INDIANA 47403
(800) 839-8640
WWW.AUTHORHOUSE.COM

First published by 1stBooks 03/11/05

ISBN: 0-7596-4605-8 (e)
ISBN: 0-7596-4606-6 (sc)
ISBN: 1-4033-5636-X (hc)

Printed in the United States of America
Bloomington, Indiana

This book is printed on acid-free paper.

...This novel is dedicated to everyone whom I ever met. However, I wanted to acknowledge some special individuals and organizations that have been very kind to me and you, the reader:

To my loving wife, who daily permits me to be myself. She's also the better half of our relationship. To my adorable son, who reminds me each day to live each day to it's full potential and carefree. To my closest friends and my four siblings, who provided me with the inspiration to become a better person--- and also bring me back down to Earth each day. To my business partner, who didn't give up on this project or me. Financially he has made this goal come true. To my co-workers, who assist me with my various work projects. To my students, who allow me to stand on my soapbox and provide insight into the American political system. They also educate me on what our nations' citizens need---and deserve.

To my parents, they gave me direction in life. Also, they enabled me to stand up for my beliefs and the self-esteem to pursue my dreams and goals in life, including writing this book.

To our servicemen and women who defend our nation and its freedoms. They voluntarily enlist to protect us and our interests in more than 120 nations across the globe. They place themselves in harms way, defending us and the abundant opportunities we enjoy as American citizens. Unfortunately, many of these rights we take for granted, including the right to express ourselves in a democratic society and the right to vote.

To the readers (and buyers) of this book, may you find the novel to be inspirational to pursue your goals in life and educational about the American political system. We live in the greatest country in the history of the world. People from across the world (including my grandfather from Ireland) have come here seeking a better life, enhanced career opportunities, and more freedoms.

Lastly, my heartfelt thanks to the staff at DuPage Medical Group (previously known as Woodridge Family Practice), the staff at Cardiac Surgery Associates, the Cardiovascular Unit at Edwards Hospital in Naperville, Illinois, Midwest Heart Specialists, and the Lord for keeping watch over me in December of 2000 and beyond. They reminded me, once again, what is truly undervalued in life---our health.

Table of Contents

Chapter One
Welcome Home!

"Bob, please come down for breakfast. Your food's getting cold," his mother proclaimed. It had been the third time she called out that morning for her nineteen-year-old son to join her in the kitchen for breakfast. Not that she looked it, but Mrs. Hamlin had grown used to her son's being late for breakfast. Like most people, she had many errands to run this Saturday morning.

Mrs. Kathleen Hamlin knew her son very well. His tardiness at breakfast, lunch, or anything in life was a bad habit he had become very good at. Motivation, organization, and dedication had not always been Robert Hamlin's strongest assets. Actually, they had very little to do with him.

As Bob finally made his way downstairs to the kitchen, it was apparent he would not be starting any new trends today. His hair was not combed, clean clothes not worn, a shower not yet taken. It was 9:40 a.m. on a Saturday morning. Bob Hamlin had returned home from school for the weekend. In doing so, he normally did the laundry, caught up on sleep, asked for money etc. All very common tasks which students like Bob were ready for and became good at doing.

Bob enters the kitchen and is immediately asked by his mother how he's doing. "Ah . . . all right, I guess," Bob replies.

"Do you miss being home?" Mrs. Hamlin asks.

"Yea, it's okay," Bob responds, giving what his mother expects from a parent - college student conversation, quickly going nowhere.

Mrs. Hamlin sits down and says, "We really need to talk about your future. Your father and I have brought this up numerous times with you, but it never seems to go anywhere." Bob's memory is not the best. However, his response as evidenced by his deep sigh, a roll of the eyebrows and by placing his forehead on the kitchen table indicates he can see where this conversation is going.

"Please listen to me!" Mrs. Hamlin shouts. "I know we have tried to talk about this before, but I think you're at a critical time in

1

your college career. You are now into your second year in college and you still have not decided on a major for your degree. Nor have you shown to your father or I ANY indication of what you may want to do with your life," she states.

Bob quickly interrupts his mother and says, "This may really surprise you . . . but very few people at school have decided on a major or a career choice at this time. Perhaps some students know what they want to do, but the number of students who have chosen a future job area for themselves is much like me. I mean, we just do not know!" he asserts.

"I know it is a hard decision to make, but have you given any thought recently to the topic?" Mrs. Hamlin calmly asks.

"No . . . not at all. My schedule this semester of psychology, finite math, and . . . geez, I cannot even remember my last two classes. My tests seem impossible and I really fear I am falling behind in my class assignments," he responds.

"I understand your school work may be hard, but some time in the future, perhaps very soon, you will have to make some decisions . . . that will affect the rest of your life. Have you picked your schedule yet for next fall?" she asks.

"No, I haven't. Registration started last week, but I didn't have the time to sit down and choose what courses I would like to take . . . but I'm OK. After this year, I will have completed all the courses (outside an academic major)," Bob answers.

"Is there anything I can do or suggest that will make this decision any easier?" Mrs. Hamlin asks.

"Unfortunately you can't. Until I finish some tests next week and finish this semester, there is not much you or anyone can do," Bob states.

"Okay, we've wasted enough time on this issue. What are your plans today?" Mom inquires.

"I have to complete one more thing in my math class. Then I have to start studying for some tests. I always seem to do everything at the last minute. . . Someday I will TRY something and start studying earlier. I am going to eat breakfast and see if I can find my books I brought home . . . I've been home what, half a day and have already lost them," Bob says.

"Oh, I'm sorry," Mrs. Hamlin says as she gets up and leaves the kitchen. "I put them here when you came home yesterday. You dropped them and then ran off so quickly that . . ."

"It's okay. I seem to lose everything . . . I think I would lose my head if it was not attached. All too often what you and everyone else say is true. It seems like I can't focus. I can't remember where I place anything. . . People must think I am a real basket case," Bob replies. The tone of his voice lowers from the sadness in his emotions. Bob sits there, looking at the floor.

"Listen to me. You are my eldest son. I have been blessed with four children, all of who are healthy, good kids. I know there are times when I get down on you. But your father and I always expect more of you because you are the oldest. Most parents do of their first child. You then, become the one we look toward when we need things done. Don't get down on yourself. Finding your future is not easy. And regardless of what happens, we will still love and support you," Mrs. Hamlin states as she kisses Bob on top of his head.

"Thanks, Mom. I'm going upstairs to get started," Bob states. He mumbles to himself while walking up the stairs. Quickly however, his mother shouts, "Hey, you will need this!" she states while holding up Bob's bag containing his books.

"Thanks," Bob says as he returns back down the stairs and retrieves his bag. "I have a lot to do . . ."

" . . . And a lot to decide," she whispers under her breath after Bob has left.

A short while later Bob is in his bedroom. He has already emptied his school bag and placed all the materials throughout the room. After doing some basic algebra problems, he stops to pause for a second. At first he is puzzled, but he realizes something is very different. On most occasions, his textbooks, papers, and folders are spread everywhere. "Something's very . . . odd," Bob states. Today is Saturday, March 30th. Even the clothes on the floor, usually located in no order, have been placed in piles pertaining to some form of rank: "clean and dirty, colored or white." Of course, his mother has spent time in between Bob's return visits home from college to clean and dust. However, even by now his room has the appearance of reality - its normal appearance once Bob has spent any time there.

After completing his algebra assignment, Bob Hamlin reads a chapter from his psychology class and prepares an outline from which to prepare for his exam in speech. Like most young adults, Bob is timid and fears speaking in public. On most occasions, his fear exceeds that of his classmates. "I don't know how people can get up there, be entirely relaxed and speak to an audience as if no one is there. God that scares me!!! I frequently have to fight myself not to vomit from being so worked up," Bob states. He shakes his head in disillusionment while reviewing a masterful performance in a televised debate between the Rev. Jesse Jackson and Rev. Jerry Falwell of the Moral Majority.

The bedroom clock reveals it is nearly 3:00 p.m. Bob has been diligently working on all the tasks he wanted to do for the past four hours. He decides to take a shower. Doing so has always helped to recharge his batteries and calm him. Besides, he has not taken one yet today. Being very self-conscious of his appearance, he discovers his afternoon of "academic adventure" has only served to decrease his attractiveness. "Man do I stink . . . whew!" Bob shouts. He decides to follow his instincts and take a shower for the benefit of humanity.

While in the bathroom, he begins to ponder all that has happened thus far today. From the placement of his books, the making of his bed, and his attention to detail, he has recognized that this is a very special, if not peculiar day. "Something's up. With the exception of any books which my Mom located, everything I need has been easy to find," Bob mumbles to himself while undressing.

After finishing his shower, he glances at the bedroom mirror. Since he has been studying all afternoon, he decides to lie down for a few minutes. By 3:45 p.m. on this Saturday afternoon, Bob falls asleep. The remainder of this particular day will leave a lasting impression on this young man from Park Forest, Illinois, a South Suburb of Chicago. Let the future begin.

Chapter Two
Facing Your Weaknesses

"Ouch!!! Man this hurts. I've told myself at least ten times not to do this but it has happened again. Every time I put more spray, gel, or cream on my face!! !. . ." Bob shouts.

"Hey, what's wrong?" Mrs. Hamlin asks, with the calm, loving voice of a compassionate mother. Once again she inquires as to what has upset her polite but very impatient son.

"My face is burning up; I put on too many creams or chemicals to fight these pimples once again!" Bob responds. "I'm getting tired of this. When are these damn things FINALLY going to go anyway?" Bob demands of his mother in obvious frustration.

Mrs. Hamlin has seen the anger in her son before, but she has realized this problem is really upsetting him. For three months now, Bob has been taking medication daily for acne. Besides the financial cost, many people have painful emotional side effects. Bleeding is frequent from the drying of the nasal tissue also. "It really affects my self-esteem," Bob whispers to himself.

"You have to remember what you put on your face. If you would just slow down, take your time, and do one task at a time . . ." Mrs. Hamlin asserts.

"I know, Mom!!!!" Bob angrily responds. "I do not need to be reminded on this topic!!! Do you really think I enjoy having to scream from the pain I'm in? This happened once again because I was stupid enough not to pay attention to what I am doing!!!" Bob shouts as he runs away.

After taking a few seconds off to observe Bob's physical and emotional status, Mrs. Hamlin pauses before speaking again. She knows, from previous experiences, that getting into a shouting match will only increase the tension between the two. She decides just to sit down on Bob's bed - hoping he will calm down.

Two minutes later, Bob reenters his bedroom. His anger eased and he has sat down beside his mother. He just stares toward the ground, obviously at a loss for what to say regarding the present situation. After a few moments, Bob mumbles, "I do not know what to do. I know I have been told many times that my face will eventually clear up, but I am having a hard time dealing with this problem. I get absent-minded at times about what I am putting on my skin because I am really frustrated with how I look . . . Having to go through high school with acne is hard."

"You are a really handsome young man," Mrs. Hamlin offers in praising her son. "I bet the young ladies at school really think you are cute."

"HA-HA-HA-HA-HA-HA," Bob laughs as he finally smiles, his face turning red from embarrassment. "Every mom says that to her son. Don't get me wrong. I can assure you, the reality of my life is right here on my face... You cannot miss it" Bob declares. He places a finger on his right cheek while emphasizing his emotions of anger and frustration. His voice then starts to crack from the tears coming down the side of his cheeks.

After a few seconds Bob regains control over his emotions. He asks his mother, "When you were younger did you have a problem with pimples?"

His mother replies, "No, Bob, I did not."

"Well, Mom, then perhaps you do not understand my situation. We have had many arguments in my life. Most of the time you have been right after all," Bob says as his mother smiles from her son's admission of error and his honesty. "But this time you do not know. I mean, I am very conscious of my appearance now. I always look into the mirror when passing it. It is not to admire, but more to think what others view when they see me. Sometimes I try to convince myself that I really do not look that bad. Sometimes it even works. But most of the time . . ." Bob offers as he sighs.

"I know you may feel bad at times, but your appearance is not permanent. You will really notice some changes in your appearance in about four to five more weeks. Bob, you are my eldest son and a really nice person. Things probably seem hard right now, but they will get better. They always do," Mrs. Hamlin calmly asserts.

"Mom, I look horrible. My face is peeling. It looks like the wrappings that fall from a mummy," Bob states.

"HA-HA-HA-HA. Bob, where did you come up with the term Mummy," his mother asks while laughing.

"I thought of it. It sounded a lot better than pizza face or crater face or. . ." Bob mumbles as he looks down at the floor again. He is sad. For two minutes silence dominates the room.

"You have to learn not to get so down on yourself. The problem you have now is going to end soon. You can be assured of that. You will look back at it sometime in the future and laugh. But more importantly, you may not realize this yet but you probably will be a better person once your blits have gone away," his mother states.

"Zits. They are zits, not blits. Besides, my face is only part of the whole picture. I really miss my favorite foods: pizza, peanut butter, and chocolate - they are all what I refer to as the basic food groups," Bob says. He begins to smile as he realizes he has just told a joke.

"Things for you seem very hard right now, but you just proved that you have a sense of humor. You turned a bad situation into an example where you can laugh at yourself . . . Be patient, Bob, things are going to get better. They always do," Mrs. Hamlin states.

"Do you really think so? Being patient hasn't been part of my life, at least as long as I remember anyway. I have always been fairly quick to react... What I have to learn to do is not react so quickly with any temper when facing bad luck, much like the problem I have with my face," Bob responds.

"How bad can it really be? It's not like you have . . . cancer or something." Mrs. Hamlin questions.

"The worst part is I feel so conscious about what people see. One glance is enough to turn away from me. Right now it has nothing to do with the chemicals, whether I shower, brush my teeth, have money to spend, etc. What hurts most is when people look toward my direction, they soon are turned off. I am having a very difficult time meeting people and making friends. When going to the mall, I end up going by myself. Right now it's really hard. I keep busy by exercising, reading, and working my two jobs. Besides going to school each day, it makes the time go by faster. When the day comes when my face has been recycled, I will be a much happier and better person," Bob declares.

"What do you mean by better, Bob?" Mrs. Hamlin inquires.

7

"Well, I have learned a few things during . . . Not only is it very personal with me, but I see it all the time with how others are treated. Today people are very rude and inconsiderate. They say things to improve their own standing among their peers, without regard to others' feelings. Believe me, I am not perfect, but this whole experience with my face has changed me," Bob mentions.

"Change? What kind of change, Bob?" Mrs. Hamlin questions, her level of interest rising with Bob's last statement.

"By being out of the loop socially, I have seen firsthand how cruel people are. Believe me; I hear a lot of rude statements about my face. People just really do not care about one another . . . I KNOW I have a severe pimple problem. I do not need to be told about it by anybody. I SEE it on my face each morning when I wake up. I have learned quite a lesson from this whole experience. When this all ends, do you know who will get the biggest hug?" Bob asks his mother.

"Me," she replies.

"No, Mom, you will get one too. The biggest one is for the pimple doctor!!" Bob states with a smile. His appreciation for both their support during the entire situation is clearly evident.

"Well, Bob, it is Friday evening. Do you have any plans tonight? What about that girl . . .? What was her name, Julie, who you were seeing?" Mrs. Hamlin asks.

"No, Mom. That ended one month ago and that was nothing. Things just did not work out. Things between girls and I seem to go okay for a few weeks, then they come to an end. I just cannot seem to keep a relationship together. Perhaps they just get bored," Bob says, offering sighs in frustration.

"Well, if that is happening, what do you think the problem is? After all, you are a handsome young man. You have your head on straight (albeit not too tight at times), usually. I think that you . . ." she states while being interrupted by her son.

"You're supposed to be polite and feel that way about me. You're my mom after all. I really don't go out much, I don't have any close friends . . . I guess that I just am not very sociable. Perhaps I am boring," Bob replies.

"Ah, come on, Bob. You may lack time from working two jobs and going to school everyday. You volunteer your time at the church, etc. Hell, with all the things you do, how can you view yourself as boring!!!" Mrs. Hamlin shouts, not trying to hide her frustration.

Bob remains quiet for a few seconds, which is rare, for he always has been quick to defend himself. He then displays a rare sense of composure, particularly for him.

"Well, most of the things I do involve a lot of time spent with people older than me. At the church, when working . . . seems like everyone is older than me. When I go to my job at the store, all the customers are older than me. Perhaps what I spend most of my time doing, most people my age do not find to be important," Bob responds with a rare sense of confidence in his voice.

"By putting it that way, you do make some sense, Bob. However, you do spend six hours a day in high school. There EVERYONE is your age. Maybe you should consider changing where you use your abundance of energy. For example, if you shifted some, not much, but a little of your time, perhaps you could decrease the problems we're talking about. You are still very young. Sure, you doubt yourself with how things seem today, but you have your whole life ahead of you. As you get older, you can work on being successful or helping people in their needs. Maybe now you should just enjoy yourself. Once you become better at it, everything else will fall into place," Mrs. Hamlin speaks while looking into the sad eyes of her son.

"Well, thanks for your advice. As usual, you are probably right." Bob realizes it is now 8:00 in the evening. "I'm going to the basement to lift some weights. I'll think more about what you said. Bye, Mom," Bob states as he departs down the stairs into the darkness.

Chapter Three
Could You, Help Me?

"Seven. Eight. Nine and ... ten. There now, all right!!" Bob shouts, while placing the weight bar back in its resting place. It rattles on the rack as Bob sinks down on the pad lying on his back. "I CANNOT believe that I finally did it. All this time I have been complaining that I could never lift it - and now I can almost bench press my weight. Gee, I did not think all this effort would ever lead to something. Perhaps if I work at the weights more often I could. . . Wait a minute. What am I saying? What am I thinking about??? Was I not there when I spoke to my Mom? Staying in on Friday night to lift weights. Yep, that will get people's attention. I'll be a real mover in the social circuit now!! I can see it now. EXTRA, EXTRA, READ ALL ABOUT IT. BOB SPENDS WEEKEND TONING UP!!" After hearing himself, Bob places his head into his hands and peers toward the cement floor in disgust. A few minutes later Bob looks up again. He is briefly startled by the telephone ringing upstairs, but he cannot find it. He decides to let his mom answer it.

It is now 8:45 p.m.

"Bob, it is for you!" Mrs. Hamlin yells down toward him in the basement. After proceeding up the stairs, he passes by his mother at the top of the stairway. "I do not recognize the voice, Bob. It is a girl," Mrs. Hamlin asserts. The smile on her face displays an obvious level of happiness for her son.

After hearing what she said, Bob chooses to take the call in his bedroom. The phone is an extension from the home's main line. "Luckily someone here installed another line so I can have some privacy. The one thing I can use my hands for is throwing them up in the air when I get angry and frustrated," Bob whispers.

He picks up the phone and clearly yells "OKAY, I HAVE IT!" into the receiver. The tenseness in his voice shows when he answers with "Hello, this is Bob."

"Hi, this is Claudia Bretz from your history class."

Although not able to show it to her by phone, but Bob is almost in complete shock. Claudia Bretz is just simply beautiful. Although a year younger, she was one of the most beautiful girls in their high school. She had blonde hair, was about 5'4" with blue eyes and a very well proportioned figure. She was shorter than Bob, who was 6'1", like most girls, but someone whose company he would CERTAINLY request at any time.

Taking a second to get over the initial shock, Bob finally speaks into the phone. "Hi, how are you, Claudia?" he responds.

"Cool . . . 'I'm glad you know who I am. Was nervous when I dialed your number, but even more fearful that you would not know whom I am. But I am glad you are home," she states.

"No, no, I know who you are," Bob replies to her while smiling. However, the entire time he was thinking to himself I KNOW who you are!!

"By calling at this time, I was not interrupting you was I? I mean, I would hate to bother you if you're already busy," Claudia mentions in a calm but polite manner.

"No, not at all. I was just downstairs lifting some weights. A fun activity for Friday night, huh?" Bob says, but he is interrupted by Claudia's laughing. "I'm done. My arms are very sore . . . What's so funny?" Bob asks.

"You are. Most people would say something like 'Oh I just arrived home from running an errand' or make up some story to impress someone. I can tell you are not lying to me because no one would say they were at home lifting weights on a Friday night," Claudia replies with a laugh.

"Me working out . . . does it bother you?" Bob asks in a nervous tone.

"No, not at all. Actually, I think it is rather cute. I mean, I asked you a question and you provided me an honest answer. You did not lie in an attempt to impress me. It could be another of your qualities," Claudia states in a rather suggestive tone.

"Oh?" Bob replies, showing the highest degree of intelligence. Playing dumb, as perceived by his peers, was not difficult for Bob. It did not require much practice either.

"Bob, I called because I wanted to talk to you about some things. I didn't know your phone number. I asked my friend Sherry how I could get in touch with you," Claudia says. Sherry Hunter was a classmate of both Claudia and Bob. She came across to most people as somewhat stuck on herself, but nevertheless, another gorgeous girl at Bob's school. "She just suggested that I look it up and I called. Here we are," she asserts in a very upbeat tone.

"You're kind of lucky it was in the book," he responds.

"Yes, WE were lucky," she answers.

"Well, Claudia . . . How can I help you?" Bob asks. He is unsure as to what she really wants or why she is calling. She soon provides the answer.

"You know, I'm not surprised to hear your offer to help." Claudia states, once again in a seductive tone. "I called for two reasons. I know you are in my history class and rumor has it you are doing very well, much better than I am anyway. I am calling because I need help in the class. I probably have an F. Would you. . . Could you help me?" Claudia nervously asks. She is unsure as to how he feels. "After all, before today we have NEVER talked before, but it seems we know who the other is," she says.

"Sure, that would be no problem, I guess. Ah, when would you want to start?" Bob questions.

"That's great. You know, I had this feeling you'd help all along. What are you doing tomorrow night?" Claudia asks him, her level of confidence being very strong.

"Tomorrow night's cool. I have to work in the afternoon. Is 8:00 okay with you?" Bob questions.

"Sure. That's fine. Would you like to come here to study? I mean it would be easier for me, since everything I need is here," Claudia replies.

"Yea, that's OK. Eight o'clock sounds great. Hey Claudia, you said there were other things you wanted to discuss with me ..." Bob reminds both him and her as to why she phoned.

"Well, to be honest, I have had kind of a problem recently. When I asked Sherry how to get in touch with you it was regarding our class because I DO need help. However, I've wanted to discuss something with you for a long time now. You see, I really think you're kinda cute," Claudia states, but she is quickly cut off by Bob.

"Come on. Give me a break. I just spent an hour tonight talking with my mom about my pimple problem. You know as well as everyone else does that I have a severe problem with acne. I really don't need someone joking with me about my appearance --- - then asking me for help with her homework," Bob angrily replies.

Claudia remains silent for a few seconds then speaks up. "You may not believe me but I know exactly what you're thinking. I understand if you're angry, but let me finish. When I was 12 or 13 years old, I had a severe case of acne too. Perhaps not the worst kind, but it really made me feel pretty insecure. I have admired you for about three months. Deep down, I am very shy and reluctant to tell someone how I really feel. It took a LOT for me to call tonight.

"The need I have for help is genuine, but it really provided me an excuse to call to speak with you. Bob, I've wanted to meet you for a long time, but the chance had never come up. I not only need help, but I really wanted to talk to you." Claudia pauses for a second, and then continues.

"I understand if you don't believe me, but I'm being very honest with you. All I am asking for is a chance to show my feelings. I mean, I really do think you're cute."

Completely at a loss for what to say, Bob replies with "Well . . . I'm very sorry. I really am sensitive about how I look. It's hard for me to trust people right now, even if they're telling me the truth. I'm really sorry that I snapped at you. Hope you don't hold it against me. Do you ... understand?"

Sure, I do. I'VE been in your situation before. Besides, I've asked around about you. Everyone agrees you are a really nice guy. Maybe people, much like I was until tonight, are reluctant to take the time to meet the real you. But I'm glad I called. I was very nervous before doing so. Tell you what. . . I will call you again tomorrow around 7:00 to give you directions to my house," Claudia patiently offers.

"Okay then, we'll talk tomorrow. . . Oh, I almost forgot. . . Uh, thanks for calling. I've always felt that you are very pretty. I never had the chance to say it either. I'm sorry I got upset. It is not every day that a beautiful girl calls me. I'll see you tomorrow," Bob asserts.

"Awwwwww. Thanks. . . That was very sweet what you said and I accept your apology," she says while hanging up. Claudia goes to sleep in obvious happiness.

"Man, I can't believe she called. I mean who would have thought it. Hey Mom, you're right. I really am ok. I do have a lot to be proud of. Things are getting better already. You won't believe who called me tonight?" Bob shouts in obvious excitement as he sprints down the hallway. Upon reaching the kitchen, he hits his head on the lower ceiling, causing him to fall. It only gave more proof of him being a happy-go-lucky, but not too bright, individual.

"Bob, are you okay?" Mrs. Hamlin shouts.

"Oh, I feel GREAT!" Bob answers while rubbing his head. "I'm going out tomorrow night. Things are getting better!! But wow, did I hit my head." He is in a much happier mood despite rubbing an area where a bump is slowly forming while walking toward his bedroom.

"That's my son," Mrs. Hamlin whispers under her breath, with a big smile on her face.

Chapter Four
Self-Examination

"Where am I? What's going on?" Bob mumbles in asking himself, not quite sure what to make of what is happening. After staring at the ceiling for a few moments, he looks around the room trying to learn what's up. "Man, what a dream I just had! What a babe she was!" Bob proclaims while stretching out on the bed. He glances over toward the alarm clock on the nightstand and sees it is 5:25 p.m. "It must be time for dinner. Better go downstairs."

Bob stands up and then proceeds toward the bathroom. He looks at himself in the mirror. His hair has a life of its own, standing straight up, after his nap. "You know, something's up. . . Something just does not seem right."

"Bob, where are you?" Mrs. Hamlin asks from the kitchen.

Bob then proceeds down the stairs very slowly, still thinking about what occurred in his previous dream.

"Oh, there you are. We'll be eating in about ten minutes. By the way, where have you been? You've been missing for. . ."

"I was doing my homework, but I fell asleep. . . Perhaps for two hours. Kind of strange, huh?" Bob responds.

"You took a NAP?" Mrs. Hamlin questions her son in near amazement. "You NEVER take naps. We have been saying for a long time that taking a nap, every so often would help you relax. How many times have we mentioned a nap would help YOU?'" Mrs. Hamlin inquires while placing her hands on his shoulders while standing behind him at the kitchen table.

"Hey. I was hoping we could talk today, but you disappeared. Were you in your room?" Mr. Hamlin asks his eldest son. "I've been outside the whole day. Had hoped you could lend me a hand," Mr. Hamlin says. A pipefitter by profession, Mr. Hamlin was well acquainted to working on their property. However, like any father he was hoping to have some help from one of his athletically fit sons.

At this time Bob's mother goes upstairs to get something. While walking down the hallway, she glances toward Bob's room and comes to a complete stop.

She pushes the door open and cannot believe what she sees. "All of his books are neatly stacked on the desk and on the floor," she mumbles. They are separated into tight piles divided by subject area. After a close inspection of the situation, she departs. Her face is charged with excitement as she goes around the corner and runs back down the stairs. Upon arrival she recognizes that Bob and his father are still talking. She decides to interrupt them by shouting, "What has happened to you . . .? Everything looks different. What is?" Mrs. Hamlin asks while being stopped by her son.

"What is what? I'm not sure what you're talking about. What have I done wrong?" Bob questions.

"Nothing. I was walking down the hall and passed your room. It was clean." Mrs. Hamlin says as she sits down, to regain her composure. "Not to be critical, but what is up? What's new? Was it your roommate? Is any GIRL involved?"

"No, not really. Just got tired of looking for lost things. So one day, I decided to start picking up after myself, putting things where they belong, etc. I even dusted the room," Bob admits to his family.

"DUST THE ROOM? You're Robert Hamlin, right?" Mrs. Hamlin gasps as she and her husband are overcome with laughter.

"How about that? Our eldest son, who never knew what a hamper was when growing up, has now become a neat freak," Mr. Hamlin jokes.

"Imagine that. Cleaning up after yourself, making your bed. . . What novel ideas!" Mrs. Hamlin says while she and her husband continue to laugh.

"Hey, you may not believe this, but I think I've been undergoing some serious changes. . ." Bob says. His younger brother Dan then cuts him off.

"Oh tell us more. Mr. Change is here. Tell us, what are you going to pull from your bag of tricks next? Please, take us to the promised land!" his brother Dan exclaims, to the laughter of his family. Dan and Bob have always fought, like most siblings who are close in age do. He is one year younger than Bob, but has always been physically stronger than he. Because of this, he frequently teases his older sibling. He could always fight off Bob's unsuccessful attempts

16

to defend him. Dan attends a private four-year college in the western suburbs of Chicago.

Bob can no longer hold back his remarks from what he has just heard, the same way he has always reacted when Dan offered his opinion when not asked. "Still go to the foot doctor college" Bob asked, which Dan's school was known for producing podiatrists. The Hamlin parents have seen where this discussion is going. They have only been there too many times before. At this time they BOTH proceed to step in before it becomes a fight. "Okay now, Bob, that's enough. You can stop. He was just teasing you, as were we," Mrs. Hamlin proclaims.

Then Bob pulls a complete reversal, for typically he would make another comment to further increase the tension. However, probably for the first time in his parents' knowledge, he ignores his brother and continues talking with his parents, as he was before his brother had walked in. He decides to avoid eye contact with Dan, treating him as if he was not even there.

"On a more positive note, I mean what I stated. There HAVE been some deep changes in my life. I've become more relaxed and even take a nap or two. I am doing better at controlling my temper when things go wrong. I know what you're thinking, however. Sure buddy; isn't happening. Your perceptions have been fairly accurate, at least until recently," Bob proclaims. At this point Dan sits down. He has grown frustrated from being ignored by his brother. Bob stating that he HAS changed apparently got Dan's attention. Rather than making a degrading comment, Dan just proceeds to eat with his family.

"For the past three to four weeks, I have not been the same person. My level of patience is up. When someone needs help, I have been more willing to lend a hand. My listening skills are getting better and I am not being so quick in pre-judging people . . .I know I will only be 20 in a short time, but I feel somewhat, mature," Bob states in a clear and poised manner to his family, much like the tone he has been showing other people recently.

"What do you think has brought about this … change that you are describing to us? It sounds great to hear." Mr. Hamlin says.

"You know, it's really strange. This semester has been very stressful. My classes are hard. I seem to spend more time studying, but getting less done. However, I don't fly off like I used to . . .I do not know what the future holds for myself, but I think it is safe to say that it will not be boring," Bob asserts.

"Future? Planning? Don't be alarmed if these words or actions surprise us. We spoke just last night. During our discussion you did not mention what careers you have considered or what you would like to do!" Mrs. Hamlin says in an impassioned plea to her son.

"Well, I didn't mention a possible career because I have not thought about it . . . I have been under a lot of school-related stress, but it has not negatively affected me a great deal. As a matter of fact, it has made me a better person," Bob offers in a dignified manner to his family.

"How is your social life going? I mean, how do you spend a typical Friday night, you stud?" his brother Dan sarcastically asks. The tone in his voice suggests he is testing Bob's newly found patience. He wants to see if he will overreact, to see what he will say. Before answering, Bob pauses to think about how to respond.

"As you already know, most college students spend their Friday nights as follows. When their last class ends, they head home. There may be a cold one awaiting them in the refrigerator (maybe even two). Happy Hour begins at 4:00, and then around 6 or 7 they return home to eat something. The typical party begins around 9:00 and 'After Hours' begins at midnight.

"I really have never belonged to a clique or been a 'lamb among the sheep'. I usually have my own thing going. But, allow me to be so kind as to answer your question. My weekend is very different from what I just explained to all of you. After my classes end, I proceed to the library. For two hours I do homework. About 5:00 I return back to the dorm and eat dinner with three to eight floor members. After dinner, I return to my room, find out what will be happening later in the evening, and then gather my books for a night of academic adventure.

"About 11 p.m. I return to the dorm after studying in the library. I shower and get dressed to go out. I either meet someone in the lobby before midnight or at the After Hours where I'll be going.

About 2 or 3 in the morning, I return home and then begin the same schedule on the next day," Bob finishes with a look of happiness on his face.

"That sounds like real excitement. Can you teach me how to be as cool as yourself?" Dan rudely asks.

"Don't look now, but you're scaring our parents. I want you to know that I have learned something. Life involves making some very difficult decisions, all of which are not always popular. There are many interests I have, all of which are more important than drinking beer or sleeping in late. Budgeting my time has become very important. From attending class, studying, socializing, and trying to enjoy myself. I'm not saying I am a purist or live a life of perfection. Nor is it THE WAY for college-age people. However, it is a path that is effective. Others could consider it as a model for how one may, not must, succeed. Based on your grade point average, it wouldn't hurt to try," Bob whispers while smiling at his brother.

"Face it, you're a dork," Dan angrily shouts. Bob just smiles at this brother treating his insult as a compliment. "Don't be too proud of yourself . . . You're a few eggs short of a dozen," Dan thinks to himself.

After Dan had calmed down, all of the members of the Hamlin family then settle in to eat a dinner prepared by their mother. Bob and Dan, despite their previous battles from the past, both share the same opinion that tonight's meal is a welcome change. "Living off dorm food becomes a real burden after a while," Bob says out loud. He, also privately contemplates if dorm food is healthy. "Why do people gain 15-30 pounds their freshman year if the food is so safe? I know the environment with the access of alcohol and late night pizzas doesn't help, but maybe healthier foods could be introduced too."

"Dan, you forgot to address a severe problem at school. We may attend very different colleges in terms of enrollment, class sizes, etc., but I am sure you'd agree that dorm food is GRADE D but edible; somewhere above dog food," Bob asserts. They, their parents, and their two younger sisters, Kara and Emily, begin to laugh.

For all individuals in this age group, the college environment produces an atmosphere for adolescent drinking. The pressure applied by their college peers, particularly on eighteen-year-old freshmen, to drink alcohol is very strong and should not be taken lightly. The pressure to go out nightly from Tuesday through Saturday is very strong. Remember, for many it is their first "taste" of freedom. On occasion they may overindulge, all in the name of having fun.

By no means does this mean that drinking by college students or the excessive consumption of alcohol by anyone should be condoned or allowed. As a matter of fact, the opposite should be true. "What the college atmosphere does, with the high level of stress placed on young people, is help to explain the abuse of alcohol among college students. But it still does not justify what is happening to us (young people) today. If the television networks, which pay schools MILLIONS of dollars showing sporting events, shifted some of the money toward curbing alcoholism among college students, maybe we could begin to address our young peoples' needs, not satisfy wants," Bob declares to the astonishment of his parents, who silently agree with him.

"Now you're on your soapbox again. Trying to deny your peers a good time. Maybe you just need to relax and go with the flow. Maybe, you need a beer!" Dan responds in anger.

"Calm down buddy. College has become is a breeding ground for partying. There's nothing wrong with having a fun time, but schools have ignored the fact that they fail to teach responsibility for one's actions and respect for one's body," Bob replies. The women present, particularly his mother, just sit there in awe of Bob's convictions. Their mouths are as wide as the oceans are deep.

The family dinner ends around 8:00 p.m. Bob remains in the kitchen to assist his mom after the others have left. "Do you have any plans tonight? After all it is Saturday," Mrs. Hamlin states in a continuation of the discussion from earlier that evening.

"Nope. I only intend to give Kevin a call at home." Kevin Chapin is Bob's roommate at school and has been so for the previous two semesters. He came home for the same reasons as Bob this particular weekend: he wanted a break. "There are a few things we need to talk about before I go to bed tonight. Other than that, no plans," Bob replies.

"When I come home I just am so tired. I do not mean to sound selfish, but coming home is a great way to relax and catch up on sleep --- while eating a FANTASTIC dinner too. By the way, thank you for the meal tonight," Bob proclaims with a very content smile on his face. Bob tries to leave, but is stopped by his mother in the hallway outside the kitchen.

"One last thing before you go. I listened with great interest to what you said at dinner tonight. Your tone, patience, and vocabulary sounded very different from our previous talks, especially our discussion this morning. You do seem VERY different from the Robert Hamlin we have all come to know in this household. Don't be upset Bob, if we, who know you best, are a little surprised by what you said during dinner. We all hope what you stated is true, but it may take some getting used to on our parts," Mrs. Hamlin relays to Bob in only the way a mother can offer to her son. "You haven't joined some cult or something, have you?" his mother intently asks Bob.

"No," he responds while laughing, "but thanks for the compliment," Bob says. "But when I do, you'll be the first to know. He walks away from his mother and goes up the stairs toward his room.

When arriving there he is very confused. He decides to call Kevin, his roommate from school. After locating the number, he begins dialing. His long-term memory is very good on most occasions. But today he could not remember it, for he had not called him at his home in over two months.

Kevin's mother answers the phone. She immediately recognizes Bob's voice and chats with him for a few minutes. She calls out her son's name and when she hears "I've got it" She hangs up. Kevin and Bob then discuss what has happened the one and a half days they have not seen each other.

Kevin, by complete surprise, asks Bob a question. Ironically it related to what Bob and his mother spoke about earlier in the day. "By the way, there is something I need to ask you. I've been meaning to say this for a while now . . . We've been living together for what, three semesters, right? During the past two months, I have noticed that your behavior has been . . . very different. Do not misunderstand me, but I've seen something. You've been treating people, say, differently from what I've seen over the past year" Kevin declares as he is interrupted by Bob.

"Do you mean rudely or improperly?" Bob inquires of his friend.

"No, on the contrary, you have been very calm, more tolerant of other people's thinking. You have not been as quick to get upset about things," Kevin says as both he and Bob laugh. "I have to ask you, what's up?"

"Well, there has been something I've wanted to talk about too. I just have been reluctant to discuss it, even though we're great friends. But since you brought it up, " Bob states as he is cut off.

"Man, I need to know. This has been EATING at me!!! Wait, brought what up?" Kevin asks, showing his consistent desire to know things. Bob has always felt he would make a great investigative reporter some day.

"I do not know what caused it, but I DO seem to be more calm and at ease with other people. What is ironic, however, is that it is occurring now. This semester has been very hard. As you know, I've been constantly on the go, do not go out as much, and I am always thinking about what assignment is due tomorrow. Nevertheless, it has NOT affected how I approach people or problems."

Kevin remains quiet as Bob continues.

"Don't know what's causing it. Maybe I'm developing a better sense of how to deal with difficult times---such as my math and biology classes. But I have discovered something that I like to do. You will not believe this, but I have gained a liking for public speaking during this semester," Bob states as Kevin offers his opinion.

"You? When we first met, you were very shy, quiet and insecure. That pimple problem of yours, I'll never forget how that hurt you. But now, you DO seem more confident about yourself. I guess it's possible that you would be a better speaker as well. And by the way, the girls have been asking about YOU. Sure they are. The parties we go to, when we eat in the cafeteria. They are all asking about

Bob Hamlin. . . You lucky stud!" Kevin says, as they both begin to laugh.

"Yea, thanks for letting me know NOW, not at the particular time or moment when the timing could be better, such as at a party," Bob replies as they both laugh. "Seriously though, thanks. My primary goal these next two months is to complete my four classes. Hey buddy, how would you feel if I were running for office someday, or if you were a spokesman on my behalf? After all, you know a lot about me and I trust you. Besides, you are very good at what you do. How does that sound?" Bob asks.

"Candidate for office. You? You know, a guy can only take so much in one day. Perhaps you may be heading off toward the deep end. Where the hell would you possibly get an idea like that? Those guys are crooks. They get criticized by the media and believe me, from what I can see they deserve it! Mr. Roommate, you are a lot better than that. The grief they place on themselves and their families' in . . . . even if they deserve it. . . Where could you get a dumb idea like that?" Kevin inquires. The tone in his voice has changed in the last two minutes.

"Ah, you're right. Perhaps I was way out on that one. I guess the thought of public speaking and being an elected official came to mind. I really have NO idea what type of career would interest me. My mom had been asking me earlier today, as she had ten times before, if I have considered a major or career field yet! As usual, I had no positive answer for her," Bob states with a sigh of disappointment at the end of his sentence.

"Well, we could all agree with your Mom there. After all, you are now near the end of your sophomore year and you still have not decided on a major. Lucky for you these academic advisors do not know the 'Hole in the wall from the hole in their you-know-what.' Otherwise the EXPERTS at our great center of learning would have thrown you out by now!!!" Kevin shouts as both he and Bob break out in laughter. Graduating from their school in four years had become a major achievement.

After a pause Bob adds, "Everyone feels it's time. Perhaps some time in the near future it will be revealed to me what I want to do with my life. Well, I've got to get going. I have some more homework to do before I go to sleep. I'll see you tomorrow at school," Bob speaks.

"Yeah, I'll see you tomorrow night! Later," Kevin replies and hangs up, while Bob slowly puts down his phone.

"Looks like I had better start doing some serious thinking about what I want to do the rest of my life. Hopefully soon I will have some clue as to what I'll want to do," Bob says as he tosses his biology textbook across the room. He turns off the lights. While lying on the bed, Bob ponders for ten minutes what had happened during the day. "SOMEDAY I will have a clue as to what I want to do when I grow up," Bob mumbles as he begins to fall asleep.

Chapter Five
The Final Exam Is Just The Beginning

It is now early May. Final Exams Week, a period that strikes fear in the heart of every college student. It is 4:00 a.m. and the alarm clock is going off. On this Wednesday morning, Bob Hamlin is trying to convince himself that everything is okay. After turning off the alarm, he lays back down while trying very hard not to yawn.

Bob has been through this before. This is the fourth edition of finals week for him. It is a very stressful time. You do not sleep very much. "Generally, if you are not eating or taking an exam, your face is stuck in a book trying to "cram" as much material into your brain. This is done not so much to learn, but to load up the brain with information to complete a test," Bob has previously thought to himself. Learning is what occurs during the semester. During finals week, you only want the output from studying to be seen as a high score or passing grade in the class.

On this morning, however, Bob is not off to the best start. This is his third day of exams and he estimates that he has gotten eight hours sleep the past three days. Between studying and insomnia - in this case the fear of not being ready to take the upcoming test - he is very tired. Failing, particularly when someone else, say your parents or the taxpayers, are paying your tuition, is a common fear among all college students. Panic attacks are frequent.

However, today poses the greatest risk, his math test.

After getting dressed, trying to eat breakfast and then doing some final math equations at the library, Bob arrives in time for the test. For some particular reason, however, Bob is very much at ease when the tests are being distributed. Throughout the exam Bob works very efficiently, doing one problem at a time. About two hours later, after looking at his watch only once during the exam, Bob hears the professor make an announcement. "Please put your pencils down, close up your materials, and turn in your tests," he states. "I cannot wait to grade them," he offers the class with the look of some evil scientist in his eye.

"I've always questioned the mental stability of that guy," a fellow student whispers toward Bob as they leave the classroom. Although Bob did not finish the entire test, he did budget his time well enough to review his work. He felt good, real good, as he departed the room into the hallway.

Mingling about, he recognizes some classmates from the math class. Many express their wish of having studied harder. Bob stated that he had done okay, but will feel better when the grades are posted. He was in the presence of those who felt they did not do well, so he did not want to rub it in. Particularly for those students who had done poorly on more than one test, finals week is a time to ponder the future. Ten minutes later Bob says goodbye and returned to the dorm.

At about 12:20 p.m. he is overcome with excitement. After arriving at the dorm, he took the elevator up to his floor, flew down one flight of stairs, fumbled the key when trying to get it in the suite door, and then sprinted toward his room. Once there, he pushed the door open and it hit the wall hard. Kevin, his roommate, was studying at the desk and was alarmed at the sight.

"AAAH, AHHHHHH, AHHHHHH!!!!!" Bob shouted for about ten seconds while standing on his bed. As he yelled, he was pounding his hands into his chest and alternating between each side. Kevin sat in shock watching Bob's act; he felt he resembled some gorilla in the jungle on the warpath. Needless to say, Kevin was VERY surprised to see what was happening. Normally Bob did not show such emotion over good news.

"Do well on your test, Bob?" Kevin asked with a look of innocence on his face.

"Three down, one to go, buddy!! I aced that damn exam!" Bob replied, pointing his finger at Kevin. "And thank you," Bob whispers while pointing his finger toward the sky.

"You can now come down off the bed," Kevin whispers. After all it was still designated "QUIET HOURS" time in the dorm. Under the rules, you are not permitted to make any noise that can be heard outside your room, or you could be "written up". Considering his success on the tests taken so far this week, Bob decided not to chance his good luck.

Since he had only finished his second year, no major job offer awaited him for the summer. Until recently, he would have let his mom call his former employer, a national chain of drug stores, where Bob had worked since high school. But this time Bob took it upon himself to call during the beginning of April, long before the mad rush began among college students to find a summer job.

"Hello Mr. Leonard . . . Yes, this is Robert Hamlin. How are you today?" Bob stated.

"Yes, Hamlin my boy, how can I help you?" he asked.

"I'm calling long distance from school. Can I return to work at the store this summer?" Bob stated.

"Well, yea. Was wondering just the other day about needing help this summer . . . Kind of surprised to hear from YOU, was expecting to hear from your Mom," Mr. Leonard says with a laugh. "Oh well, you must be maturing . . . getting older," Mr. Leonard offers.

"Yes . . . Yea, I guess so. Thanks for the compliment, sir. I will call in another month," Bob declares.

"OK. We'll talk to you soon!" Mr. Leonard says. After hanging up the phone, he whispers to himself "I KNEW that young man had a clue . . . Maybe he just plays dumb."

During the previous year, Bob also began to realize the importance of effective communication. He did find some literature he used to prove his point of view. He read an article printed in one of the daily newspapers in Chicago. The article described a recently published book where the author was very critical of the communication skills of people ages 19 to 35. The author felt that young people do not fully recognize the importance of talking with one another.

"The author argued how young people were losing out on both business and personal relationships, all because they were either too busy or too PROUD not to return phone calls - or acknowledge a card or letter they received," Bob summarized to a group of 3-5 people from his college suite late one evening. In the final analysis, the author concluded that young adults who chose to follow up on those contacts made while in a business or social setting would be those people most likely to succeed.

"FINALLY someone else understands what I've been saying for the past three years," Bob declared to himself after his floor mates left. The article confirmed his previous beliefs about communicating as valid. He came to believe that his line of reasoning, often disputed and poked fun of by others was really correct.

Eating dorm food and drinking a lot of beer had caused him to gain about 25 pounds during his first year. On a personal note, Bob noticed there was something VERY wrong with his body. He was very uncomfortable with his shirt "tucked in" while sitting in lecture hall. His stomach was pressing against one end of his desk. Sitting in those small desks soon became a chore. At first he denied there was a problem . . . But now, he could not even tuck in his shirt. "This is damn pathetic . . ." Bob stated. "If I don't start taking care of myself, some nurse or doctor will have to . . . look at me," Bob shouted while looking at himself in the mirror.

As the summer progressed, his level of confidence, maturity, and appearance all began to increase and the bulge began to disappear. His ability to communicate had improved primarily from the use of his social skills. His part-time job enabled him to socially interact with people more frequently. "Dealing patiently with people is a difficult task. I've become good at dealing with bad people," Bob stated. He had just helped to escort some drunk from the store.

Bob soon gained another means to express himself by writing. Over time, as he developed a greater sense of security in who he was and what he believed in, he became more comfortable sharing his views with other people. "Being able to document your material is very important for everyone, but even more so for young people like myself. After all, people rarely take us seriously. . . But if we can show that we are responsible in our actions and the beliefs we hold dear, then perhaps a little more respect could be forthcoming. Since young people lack life experiences, being able to demonstrate knowledge with numbers, facts, etc. was even much MORE important," Bob conveyed while meeting one weekday evening with the priest of the church on campus.

Much like everyone else, summer came to an end much too soon. After much soul searching, few people discover what they want to do during their lives. As Bob's level of confidence improved, his willingness to pursue such a quest increased as well. "Someday, with a certain amount of luck, maybe I could be ready to step forward and face the challenge," Bob declared. . . "Who would ever give some college student the chance?"

Chapter Six
Go Out and Enjoy Life. You Only Live Once

"Come on, Bob, let's get going!" someone yells while knocks are heard at the door.

"YEA, MAN, IT'S TIME TO PARTY!!!" another shouts.

A third offers, "It's time to show the people on this campus who the real studs are!"

Bob puts down his pen on the desk as he hears additional knocking on the door. The same voices are heard shouting some familiar lines questioning his masculinity. Outside his door, a few of his floor mates are calling for him to come so they can all go out. This Boys' Night Out has become a ritual on their floor and most college dorms. Up until a few weeks ago, he would have been more than willing to go perhaps even leading the cheers for others to go. Oddly, his level of desire had shifted toward studying and other activities.

"COME ON, THE NIGHT IS STILL YOUNG."

"BOOOOOOBBBB!!! LET'S GO!! Some people yelled.

The door to enter their twelve-person suite opens and it is Bob's roommate Kevin. He had gone to an earlier social function, but had returned to go out with his floor mates. They had all hoped Bob would join them for the evening. Privately a few thought he was missing out on too many "nights out" to relax and enjoy himself.

"Good to see you buddy," one stated.

"We are really glad you are home. We KNOW he is inside, but he will not open the door. Can you ask him to get ready so we can go out?" one asks.

"Yea, get him out here. We are tired of his excuses about him being busy. Tell him to get his," another states as Kevin cuts him off.

"All right guys. I get the picture. Sit down, relax, and I will go in and see if Bob is in there," Kevin says.

"We KNOW he's there. He has not left since dinner. Let's. . ." a third floor mate declares.

"Guys! I know. Give me a few minutes to take care of this. Let me talk to him. Besides, I have wanted to talk with him for a while," Kevin replies, the last sentence said under his breath.

As Kevin opens the door, he motions to the others to remain seated. He does know what the others may not. He's been working on a term paper from earlier in the day, which is due in two weeks. But nevertheless, he also knows it is due in two weeks, not two days. He has become frustrated with Bob. The two rarely do anything together anymore. After a brief moment to think, he comes to the conclusion that Bob will be going out and joining them on this evening.

"Hey, how are you?" Kevin asks. The two not only are roommates, but have become very close friends as well.

"It's not too bad. I just wish I had more time tonight. If I did I could finish this in a few hours," Bob replies in a rather sad tone, as he continues to write.

"Hey . . . the guys and I were talking. We all think you should join us tonight. I know you have a lot of work to do, but perhaps it could be a good idea to go out. After all, we'll have a good time," Kevin says.

"Well, this paper is very important and it still needs a lot of work. I think that. . . "Bob says as he is cut off. As he spoke, he continued to write.

"I want to make something perfectly clear. Over the past year, I have watched you very closely. You are more mature, you look great with all the exercise you do, and the level of self-confidence you now have is evident to everyone. In terms of improving yourself, I only wish I had your dedication to work on my weaknesses. . .You're now going to do something for the others outside the door AND for me," Kevin states politely while removing the pen from Bob's hand. "For the past month you have been a hermit. You live in this room or in some corner in the library. We don't do ANYTHING together anymore, except eat.

"I have not said anything until now, but you're really beginning to piss me off," Kevin declares in a loud and clear voice. Kevin's tone scares Bob, for he has never seen him upset before. Kevin stares right at Bob, either trying to make sure his point is understood or to regain his composure. About a minute later, Kevin begins talking again.

"Now, I'm going to politely ask you to put the books and materials away, to take a shower, and get your ass dressed. We're going out and you have an appointment to join us . . . I'll be out in the suite," Kevin says with a stern look on his face. Ironically, he then smiles at Bob, opens the door, and leaves the room, quietly closing the door behind him.

"Guys, I want you to relax," Kevin says, while placing his finger over his lips, asking for quiet from the others. "He will be coming out very soon."

Sure enough, two minutes later the door opens and Bob comes out. He is wearing a bath towel and carrying some toiletries. "Hey. I need to take a quick shower. . . Thanks for the free tip. Once again, you've proven me wrong," Bob states with a growing smile as he shakes Kevin's hand in a firm grasp. Their respect for each other is clearly visible as shown by their embrace.

One floor mate earns a chuckle from the sight of the two young men hugging by saying, "Are you two SURE you want to go out? I mean, if you both prefer to stay in tonight and have some private time alone together, just let us know."

The others there begin to chuckle, but are silenced by the stares from both Bob and Kevin. After everyone had stopped, Bob and Kevin break out in laughter of their own. The tension, which had been growing between the two of them, has been lifted.

Within a few minutes Bob is dressed and ready to go. These five friends all begin their way toward Sparky's, a singles bar on North Street conveniently located next to most of the other bar sites in the downtown area. North Street is five blocks south of what is commonly referred to as The Strip, a collection of apartment complexes where most of the students under 21 years of age go to socialize.

Cullerton is one college town where the underage drinking laws are strictly enforced. As the five are walking to the bar, one of them brings up the issue of the perceived harshness the town members have towards the students. "We bring them all this money and for what? They have shown they do not care about us," Gary states.

Ironically, as he finishes his speech, the five all witness one of their peers get arrested, most likely for public urination.

As the others join Gary in their criticism of the town's strict laws, Bob starts to consider what they are discussing. However, he looks at it from a different perspective. When he arrived at their school in Central Illinois, Bob's opinion was in agreement with how his friends feel. But over time, he noticed there were two sides to this story. He learned how the townies' homes were situated often next to a fraternity house or a large apartment building. "At first I felt it was kind of like moving next to an airport then complaining about the noise," Bob thinks to himself.

Later he began to think, "Gee, you know if I lived here I would not appreciate this either. We students come in here for eight months at a time. After a long night of partying, we'll walk home stone drunk and relieve ourselves on someone's front lawn or on their property." Bob came to agree that there was room for improvement in the relationship between the townspeople and the students. "Maybe if we didn't act like drunks, we wouldn't be treated as idiots by the townspeople," Bob whispers to himself.

The discussion about the town's laws continues until they reach the bar. At Sparky's they discover a long line at the door to get in. Like the other students ahead of them, they must patiently wait their turn. Luckily the weather is fantastic with the temperature being 58 degrees, warm for an evening in the beginning of April. Their topic of discussion now shifts from local politics in the town to the young ladies waiting in line ahead of them.

Sparky's is a singles bar. It has a reputation for being a place to "meet" someone if you want to get lucky. After a long wait that lasted nearly an hour, the five guys all enter the bar shortly after 10:00 p.m. Because many students at the bar are regulars they soon recognize some friends and classmates from school. They approach the bar area. Their immediate quest: find an available empty pitcher. Locating an empty table, also, proves fruitless as well, so they must all stand.

By this time, now 10:15 p.m., things are really beginning to jump. The dance floor is jam-packed and the emotion level is high. The outfits are revealing and the booze is flowing! With the exception of the long wait at the bar to buy a beer, which seems like forever, things are perfect. The young ladies of course, have a more serious complaint: The long line for the bathroom. It extends out the door, past the DJ booth twenty feet away, and towards the direction of the men's washroom. "This is an issue of common sense that has continued for too long and, as a problem, men should easily support," Bob whispered to Kevin.

"Where do these ideas come from?" Kevin asks in stunned response.

After what seems like forever, the five friends gather together again after buying another round of drinks. While talking to Bob, Kevin interrupts his friend to make clear that SOMEONE has earned their attention.

"Wait a minute buddy. May I direct your attention to a gorgeous female? She, I might add, is staring at you," Kevin states while placing his hands on Bob's left shoulder.

"Oh yea, where?" Bob replies, suddenly his interest level has rise.

"About 11:00 from your left shoulder, perhaps twenty feet away," Kevin answers in a code generally reserved between the two of them.

As Bob looks toward his left, he identifies the target of Kevin's affection. She is staring right at and practically THROUGH Bob.

"You have that eagle eye again tonight!!! A direct hit, I may add," Bob replies to Kevin while staring at the young lady.

The woman the two speak of is simply beautiful. She is about 5'6" tall, weight of about 120 to 130 pounds, with a body that could stop a clock. She has very firm thighs, blonde hair, blue eyes, large breasts, and a beautiful smile. Bob realizes he has seen her before, but at the immediate time he cannot remember where.

"You're right buddy, she is beautiful," Bob states in a polite but confident voice.

The young lady briefly glances back toward her friend for a moment and laughs then returns to staring at Bob. Kevin turns to his roommate and says, "Perhaps you should go over and introduce yourself."

Bob asks, "Do you think so?" the tone showing a lot of uncertainty.

"Yes, I think it would be the politically correct thing to do," Kevin responds. Bob recently declared what his major was: Political Science. Kevin places his arm around Bob's shoulder and states, "I will be right here waiting for you. Go. . . and make me proud."

Bob hands his beer to Kevin without taking his eyes off of the young lady before him. He slowly walks toward her, focusing on his own posture: head up, shoulders back. Being ever the gentleman, Bob addresses the beautiful young woman before his eyes by saying "Pardon me, would you mind if I spoke with you for a few minutes?"

She replies, "Yes, but only for a few minutes." A smile forms on her face as the two move slightly away from the elevated wall encircling the dance floor. The noise at the bar is VERY loud, so moving will better enable each other to hear. Both smile as they laugh from her response a moment before.

"Since my time is limited, let me introduce myself. My name is Bob Hamlin. . ." Bob replies while being interrupted by her during the middle of his sentence.

"I know who you are. You used to come here every Friday and Saturday night, but I have not seen you in a while. I have a close friend who has two classes in Cannon Hall (the building which contains the political science department). She knew you from a previous class you both had. One day I saw you speaking with her as I approached. . . I asked who you are. By the way, my name is Tracy," she replies.

"You've seen me before?" Bob politely asks.

"Uh, more than once," Tracy answers with a smile.

"Well if that's true, why haven't we?" Bob attempts to ask her.

"Perhaps the timing was not right," Tracy answers while cutting him off. She is infatuated with him, but wanted him to know who was running the show, at least tonight. Everything in life happens for a reason or a purpose. Just because we see each other does not mean we'd ever meet. Look around; there are a lot of beautiful women here tonight, right?" Tracy asks as Bob looks around the crowded nightclub. "How many girls here would you like to meet and team up with? Don't play dumb, Bob, I know what college guys want," Tracy asks in a seductive tone. After all, you just don't walk up to everyone at a bar and introduce yourself to each person you come across, do you?" Tracy asks while smiling.

Bob replies, "I . . . plead the Fifth." He was referring to the Fifth Amendment of the U.S. Constitution, prohibiting forced testimony against oneself, as she laughs.

"No, perhaps at a party where it is easier to meet people, but not at a bar. I'm glad we finally had a chance to meet . . . Perhaps we can get to know each other better," Tracy says.

The two of them chat for about half an hour when Bob asks, "You were standing near the railing 'people watching' before we met. Would you like to dance?"

"Sure . . . but just for a few minutes," she answers as they both laugh. They proceed to the dance floor holding hands. After eight songs together there, the announcement 'Last Call' is made by the bartender. Bob turns toward Tracy and says, "I had a great time tonight. . . Would you like to go somewhere else?"

Tracy places her arms around him and replies, "Not a chance. . . I really had a great time too, but I don't go home with guys the first night. But, here's my phone number. I'll be mad if you don't call me tomorrow."

"Tracy, I'll call you TONIGHT when I get home," Bob responds.

"No, don't. If you call, you may wake up my roommates. It wouldn't be a good way to build upon a VERY favorable first impression," Tracy declares with a smile.

"Well. . . I may choose to do it anyway," Bob says with a big smile on his face. He gives her a kiss on the cheek and wishes her good night. They say goodbye in the presence of Bob and Kevin's floor mates with a long romantic hug. . . looking deep into each others eyes. The expressions on their faces indicate they are DYING to know what has happened.

"Man, where did she go?" Kevin inquires. He is trying to learn why she and Bob did not go somewhere else that evening together.

"Who is she? What's she like?" "She's hot!!!" the others ask, joining their friend Kevin in asking Bob.

"Her name is Tracy. We got along great. She's fantastic. . . I'll be calling her tomorrow," Bob responds.

"Tomorrow Bob? We were all wondering about TONIGHT!" a friend asks as the others all show their agreement.

"I know what you guys are thinking," Bob declares. "I thought the same thing too, but she is, different. I mean, she's wonderful."

"Oh, that's GREAT. Do you think you are falling in love again?" Tony, one of their floormates, yells much to the entertainment of everyone present. Even Bob begins to laugh. However, Bob did not answer the question. He was too occupied watching Tracy leave the bar. She waved back at him while walking out the door. The five young men proceed to return to their dorm, laughing both at Bob and at themselves.

"She really was . . . different," Bob mumbles under his breath. "I will call her tonight anyway."

"Did you say something?"

Chapter Seven
Seeing the Big Picture

After arriving home at the dorm, Bob was very clear in letting his roommates know he had a great time at the bar. "Guys, I just want to say thanks for bringing me out with you tonight. I had a lot of fun," Bob speaks.

"You're up here talking as if you won an academy award for being a STUD or something. Just sit your ass down," Eric says. He is a member of their floor who did not go out with the others tonight. Everyone laughs as they lightly tease Bob. They should not be misunderstood. They really DO like Bob, but they just like to play with him for always being so proper and gullible.

"Yea Bob, lighten up. I mean you went out tonight. We were there. We went out too. It's obvious from what you are saying that you . . . enjoyed yourself. You met some gorgeous babe," says Tom, who lives in triple---a room occupied by three people.

"Just promise us you won't fly solo tonight!!!" John yells to the howling laughter of his floor mates.

"Seriously, what is she like?" Kevin asks with a smile as the guys continue to tease Bob.

"Well, all things aside, she is simply beautiful and very intelligent," Bob replies.

"Bust and brains. Way to go buddy!" Eric shouts as the others laugh.

"Don't forget you have a Mother. Besides, you're good at being an ass," Bob answers. His tone is low, but it is evident he is not very happy. Eric jumps up, but is restrained by Tom and his roommate. A few moments later he sits back down. Eric likes to believe he controls the floor, but recently Bob and the others have been trying to "ease his responsibilities."

"Roommate. . . They're just teasing you," Kevin says. "Seriously guys, Bob made the time to go out with us tonight. He has been working on some huge paper recently, like he ALWAYS is, while all we can do is poke fun of him. Hey, it was good to see you in action again tonight," Kevin says while slapping his roommate on the back. His happiness to see Bob join the social circuit instead of swimming in schoolwork is clearly visible.

"Well guys, I am going to bed now. See you at lunch tomorrow," Bob says.

"Be sure to say high to Tracy for me. She really seems nice," Kevin offers. The others do not understand what he means but Kevin knows that Bob will probably be making a phone call very soon.

Bob tosses his clothes onto the floor after entering the room. He picks up the phone and relaxes on the bed. Kevin is not a tarot reader. He just knows Bob very well. Sure enough, he pulls out Tracy's phone number and begins dialing. Just before the second ring, a voice is heard at the other end.

"Hello," a young female states in answering the phone.

"Hi, is Tracy there?" Bob asks.

The voice at the other end begins laughing. After a few seconds, she responds, "Hi Bob, this is Tracy."

"Hi. . . Wait, how did you know it was me?" Bob asks with a strong sense of innocence.

"My roommate Sharon heard your offer to call when we were at the bar. She thought it was . . . odd. She teased me about it while we were walking home together," Tracy states.

"So, when coming home, there was some discussion about me, huh?" Bob inquires with a look of happiness on his face.

"Stop glowing stud. I can hear that smile on your face from here, even over the phone. Yea. . . We talked about you. And, before you ask, I found you to be very different from most other guys," Tracy says. The sound of Bob's laughter briefly interrupts their chat.

"I'm sorry. . . I don't mean to laugh, but that was the same answer I gave when they asked about you tonight. Don't be offended but . . . you're very attractive," Bob declares while laughing.

"Thank you," she replies with a genuine sign of appreciation in her voice.

"You're also very educated and intelligent. From the subjects we were discussing, it was easy to see you really have a good head on your shoulders. Besides, you have got a GREAT body as well" Bob offers in a clear and confident manner.

"Thanks. By the last statement I know you are being VERY truthful."

They both laugh.

"You know, I get 'hit on' a lot. It's not too often I open up to someone like I did tonight . . . with you," Tracy says.

"Why me then?" Bob asks with a great deal of curiosity.

"As I said earlier there's, a time and place for everything. I was really hoping you'd be there tonight," Tracy whispers so her roommates would not hear.

"Oh," he answers with a complete sense of stupidity. They both laugh.

"Besides, I did win a $1 bet from Sharon. I had bet her that you would call tonight," Tracy states while laughing.

"Even though you told me not to?" Bob asks.

"Well, you had to," Tracy replies. "Besides, I would have lost my bet if you didn't."

"Okay, Babe! Using me already for a lousy dollar. Fine, .a lot of faith you have in me. Maybe dollar should be my nickname for you," Bob shouts as they both laugh.

Their discussion continues for fifteen minutes before she finally asks him "By the way, what's your phone number? I had a great time tonight."

"If I give you my number, would you mind if we got together tomorrow, perhaps for dinner?" Bob asks with a degree of hope the answer will be positive.

"Sure. Dinner would be a great idea. How about 7:00 p.m.?" she requests.

"That'll be great. It will allow me to finish my homework," Bob responds. "I had been working on a term paper the entire day before going out tonight. The ONLY reason I went out is because my roommate and some guys on the floor applied some not too subtle pressure to go out to the bar. Kevin, my roommate, is of the opinion I spend too much time working on my school work and not enough time enjoying myself" Bob relays to Tracy.

"Do you think he is right?" she asks.

"I really don't know. Perhaps spending a lot of time doing homework on something you believe in is not a BAD idea after all.

However, I will tell you this. If you intended to go out tonight and meet some guy who has a poor sense of organizational skills, who lacks direction, well then I have some really bad news for you. I AM NOT THE GUY FOR YOU," Bob states to her.

"No, I wasn't planning to meet anyone. I'd seen you before. Was hoping to see you sometime. But I do appreciate your honesty. It's, a welcome change. However, it's late. I had a lot of fun tonight. I'll see you about seven tomorrow, okay?" Tracy inquires.

"Yea sure. I'll call you sometime tomorrow. I had fun tonight. Good night, Trace," Bob says.

"Thanks. You're really. attractive too," she whispers to him with a seductive tone in her voice.

"Need to return the phone back where it was. I don't want to raise any suspicions that I would call her," Bob states. He turns off the light and lies down with his arms crossed behind his head. Bob begins to review the events over the course of the last five hours with a very happy look on his face. "She really is different," he states. "I hope my unusual habits do not scare her off. I really need to let things just happen in my life. . ."

Bob now realizes that he has awakened from a dream. The view in the room is nothing but darkness. Everything is in the same position it was just two hours before when he had gone to sleep. At 12:24 a.m., everything is peaceful in their home in the South Suburbs of Chicago. There is a certain aura about the place from the events that have just passed. He flips over on his side to consider what has been happening the last two hours.

The events in the dream were very satisfying. "Meeting a beautiful blonde who finds me attractive does not happen each day. However, I don't understand what's happening in my sleep tonight. In what direction am I being pulled?" Bob asks. After waking up from his dream, he thinks about the discussion he had with his mother earlier in the day. He's always been honest with others, but more importantly, he has begun to practice being more honest with himself.

Still not sure what purpose lengthy term papers or political science has in his life, he lays back down. Upon going back to sleep at 12:45 a.m., he magically returns to a plot his mind has him playing tonight.

"So Bob how are you and Tracy doing? You have been dating for nearly a year now, is that correct?" Mrs. Hamlin asks.

"Yes, it will be a year on April 22nd, about two weeks after we first met. Things are great. We're both very busy with school. Since we do not live in the same building, we do not have the chance to see each other as much as we would like. She's. . . special," Bob replies. He has returned home for the weekend for a Saturday night dinner at home. His parents and Dan, his brother, join him at the kitchen table.

"You know Bob, there is something your mother and I wanted to speak to you about. We have been discussing a subject in your life that will affect your long-term future," Mr. Hamlin remarks to his eldest son. The calm and serious tone in his father's voice was always effective to get and hold the attention of the sons in the Hamlin household. Thomas Hamlin was both the income earner and disciplinarian in the household. He did not speak much, but when he did, he addressed issues of concern to the Hamlin family. On most occasions, Mr. Hamlin's seriousness of speech easily attracted the focus of Bob and the other children of the family.

"Like I stated, Son. Your mother and I have done some talking recently. We wanted to address the subject of your relationship with Tracy. Do you think you will be together for the long haul?" Mr. Hamlin asks.

"I don't understand. What are you referring to?" Bob asks in response to his father's - and indirectly his mother's - question. From previous experience, Bob can see what direction this conversation is headed, but prefers to play dumb. Doing so permits his parents the courtesy to ask and offer opinions of how they feel.

"We don't want you to misunderstand or misinterpret what we mean. Don't make the mistake of getting all upset with how we feel. We really DO like Tracy. She is a very attractive and sweet girl. However, our concerns primarily are of a long term religious nature regarding your relationship," Mrs. Hamlin states in the presence of the others.

"I'm sorry, but what are you really referring to?" Bob inquires. His brother Dan is sitting there with a strong sense of anticipation, waiting for Bob to get upset and let his emotions get the better of him. He looked like a tiger waiting for his prey.

"Your father and I were born and raised up in the Catholic faith. We have always tried to give our children what they want, often at great sacrifice to ourselves. We feel that one of the reasons our marriage has succeeded, where many others have failed, is due to our strong religious beliefs. In fact, our religious backgrounds are very similar. For example, we still attend church together each Sunday. Your father and I wanted to ask if you and Tracy have had any talks about your future, such as getting married?" Mrs. Hamlin calmly asks. She is expecting an outburst from her son.

Dan now waits for his brother to erupt." However, Bob begins to laugh, the intensity of it increasing with each passing second. After about thirty seconds, he regains his composure, only after fully realizing that his parents are VERY serious and they're not laughing. Even his brother begins to sit back and fold his arms, wondering why Bob is laughing at all.

"I am sorry, Mom. I really am. By no means am I trying to offend you. I've been sitting in my room writing a term paper for my state government class the whole afternoon. After four hours, most of it wasted, I began to wonder how I was going to finish this semester. I have five political science classes. Nobody has done that before at our school. In fact, doing so isn't allowed by the powers that be. . . They must have been asleep at the wheel when they let me do it."

"I understand your concern and desire for me to give more serious thought for my future. We've talked about this issue countless times. The main priority for me is just to take one day at a time and complete my school assignments, while trying to survive this semester . . . As for Tracy and I, you know I really like her. She is a fantastic girlfriend AND friend. She is an extremely beautiful person. Her attractive appearance is evident but she really does care about people. She is ALWAYS there for me. And like most of the other females at our school, she is studying to be a teacher.

"Her level of concern and patience extends not only to me, but to everyone else she meets. Believe me, I could do a lot worse in dating someone else. Based on the time we have spent together, I would be hard pressed to improve myself by even trying. In fact, I'd probably be wasting my time doing so," Bob declares

"Regarding the idea of getting married. . . I do know how you feel. I understand your opinions about marrying someone who shares the same religious preference or beliefs we do. You are correct in your observation that marriages had better success rates in the past - and a POSSIBLE reason for that happening was that people were of the same religion.

"However, look at our own extended family. There have been two marriages that ended in divorce among our relatives. And both of them were blessed within the Catholic faith. Nothing, regardless of how sacred it is, is etched in stone or lasts forever," Bob asserts.

"I've always believed that when I was prepared to settle down and thought I had found the person I was going to marry, it would be without a requirement as to what religion she was, practiced, or what she prayed for and to whom. We all have opinions and other ways, including our actions, not membership cards, that identity us and reveal who we are and what we stand for. Please Mom and Dad, let me finish. I know you want to jump in and contest what I have stated," Bob declares in a firm voice. He does not mean to disrespect his parents so he quickly regains his composure.

"I know what I think is not the majority opinion in this house. But please you must learn something . . . You cannot live my life for me. It is my decision as to what I do, now and in the future," Bob states, his voice fading as he finishes.

"But most people get married to someone of the same faith son. Why? Because doing so works. It's not because they have to. If it isn't broke, don't fix it," Mr. Hamlin asserts.

"Dad, it worked because marriage, like work roles, were given by tradition. Whether for better or worse, ironically part of the marital vows a couple takes at the wedding service, the world has changed. Perhaps it is worse today, but young people do not automatically follow in what their parents did before them," Bob offers.

"Young people today. . . They just don't know how things work or are too stubborn to see what has ALWAYS worked," Mrs. Hamlin states in a higher voice.

Before continuing, Bob pauses to gather his thoughts. He then proceeds with the discussion. "Mom, consider your statement 'has always worked.' Young people today are the victims of increasing violence and higher divorce rates from the Baby Boomers' generation. Many of these people were Catholic as well. Describing how marriage has worked best is not necessarily true. Unfortunately, a result of young people getting married today is that they have improved the process of divorce. By no means did they invent it," Bob asserts in a calm voice.

"How can you say that?" Mr. Hamlin asks in a louder tone of voice.

"The proof you seek is easily available. Just visit the divorce section of any county government in the COUNTRY. The record will show the numbers of divorced marriages increased in the late 1970's. Kramer vs. Kramer was not the movie of the year in the early 1990's. It won the award about fifteen years earlier because it was a film people could relate to. The numbers then skyrocketed in the early 1980's and have since declined with each year. Why? Because most of the people who have considered filing for divorce to resolve their marriage differences have now done so," Bob says.

"There you go again, being a computer. You have a number for everything. Why can't you just talk like everyone else, instead of being a computer!" his brother Dan says. It's been awhile since he joined the discussion. He was busy in eating tonight's dinner. Bob just stares at his brother for ten seconds and smiles, dismissing what Dan just said as being unimportant.

"Statistics. . .they do tell us something. If we were to read some of the divorce files, perhaps scan through some orders of protection; we may learn that in each example, here were two people that probably should never had gotten married in the first place. The key problem, of course, is that on too many instances, children were made to suffer. . . I'm sorry, but difference of religion just is not a legal or common sense cause for divorce," Bob states while trying to defend his position in the same restrained tone as when he began.

His parents probably do not recognize his composure at this time. Unfortunately, they are too concerned with what Bob stated, not how he came across in his delivery.

"Then why are marriages failing today when they succeeded in the past? I bet you think you know this answer as well!" Mrs. Hamlin loudly states to the other members of the family. Everyone responds by laughing to what she said, everyone except for Bob.

After gathering his thoughts, Bob addresses the family by stating "I can only offer a possible answer. Contrary to what you all may think, I don't know everything. A, but not the, reason they succeeded was that financially the woman was more dependent upon her husband. She stayed home all day raising the children and maintaining the home. The man had the primary role of being the breadwinner."

"Today due to progress or financial necessity, both are employed outside the home. Women have slowly gained in their chances for career opportunities, income and education levels. . ."

"Women do not earn the same as men Bob! Where do you come up with that?" Mrs. Hamlin angrily questions her son.

"I didn't say that. There are greater opportunities for women today than ever before. She doesn't have to be Mrs. Cleaver from the 1950's TV show. With higher salaries today in terms of both value and percentage, women today are not always forced to remain in a marriage where they are not happy, or sadly, being physically abused. At least today, she has a better chance to have a choice to leave a dangerous marriage. Thirty years ago the option wasn't available," Bob states. He starts now to eat his dinner. Up until this time, he had not touched it.

His parents remain quiet for a few moments. Bob concludes they must be thinking, for he is smart enough to know they do not agree with him. Mr. Hamlin then speaks to address the family once again.

"We do not intend to argue with you. We only wanted to express how we felt about continuing in your religious faith."

"I really haven't been thinking about marriage . . . Right now I am trying to complete this semester so I can graduate in May," Bob politely responds.

"Not to change the subject, I have decided to go to law school. Since I have no serious job offers when I graduate, returning for graduate work made the decision a lot easier. After I complete law school, in debt to the level of my neck," Bob states while raising his arm to show how high that really is. After all, he is 6'1" in height. "I have no idea what to do afterwards. Maybe I'll get into politics or be a writer. . . I don't know yet," Bob speaks to his family.

"Law school? How will you ever afford it? Money does not grow on trees you know," Mrs. Hamlin states.

"Politics?" his father asks. "You've got to be kidding?"

"Well, I don't know. . . However, regardless of what I do in my life, or how many times I appear on TV or regardless of how successful I become. . . I will not fail because I did not try my best at whatever I attempted. I'm a lot like that famous bunny, still going. I never get tired. I am the Epitome of Motivation!" Bob declares with his arm extended, a rare display of confidence. It surprises his family.

"The what of what?" his brother Dan asks in response.

Chapter Eight
Graduation Day

Everyone had opened their gowns and passed the monitors' No presence of alcohol test. After what seemed like forever, the 1,000-plus graduates of the College of Sciences and Arts parade in and assume their seats in the arena. Bob had nicknamed it "the spaceship." It was largely financed and built by the fees paid per semester by the 21,000-plus students at the school. Regardless of whose name was on the building, today the building and the world was theirs.

After finally getting situated, the large graduating class becomes awake with the arrival of the first speaker of the program, Dr. Laura Camms. She is the Dean of the College of Sciences and Arts. Bob had always hoped that at his graduation, he would be lucky to hear some inspirational words of leadership and congratulatory notices from the world. However, the first speaker proceeds on a path Bob and others did not quite anticipate on this day.

"As you sit there today, I am sure you have many thoughts running through your mind. Many of you are thinking about the fun times you had here. Perhaps some of you are thinking about Wall Street or all the money you will earn in the years ahead. Maybe the idea of not seeing your friends anymore or how you will pay off your student loans has crossed your minds. Hopefully, at least in the future, all the knowledge and insight you have gained in your studies here will be there when you need it."

"However, folks, I have some bad news after all: your degree will soon be worthless. The countless hours of studying the material you learned, particularly the exams you crammed for, the endless documents you photocopied, etc., all were for nothing. Studies now show that the money you have spent here the last four or five years may not have been the most wise investment to make," declares Dr. Camms.

"Thanks ma'am. Where were you five years ago when I stood in line for hours waiting to enroll for that class that was cancelled TEN minutes before I got to the front of the line?" shouts one member of Bob's graduating class.

"You could have saved me the last five years of my life," another shouts as the graduates around him all yell similar remarks.

The responses from the graduates continue despite the dean resuming her speech. Perhaps everyone would not be as rude and interrupt if they felt she had something relevant to say. After all, this is an important day in their lives.

"Who the hell is she? The greatest day in my life and she says the money and stress were for nothing. What nerve!" someone shouts.

The loudest response came from the last student to respond to her remarks. "What does she mean about our degrees being meaningless? Hey babe! Don't you dare tell me you like to be called Doctor and do not get any thrills for it. She works for this university and tells us the last four years of OUR lives were meaningless. Who is this. . .bitch?" he yells as the students roar in applause.

". . . And I would just like to state one more item in closing," the dean states. The graduates love it. After all, more than half of them stand to applaud, drawing the anger of the university president. As she departs, it would be an understatement to reveal they were happy to see her leave. Thunderous cheers of joy erupt from the graduates. "Many of the guests feel the graduates were impolite, but here is the tiebreaker: it is our day to rejoice, not the dean's day to sober them up," Bob mumbles to himself. He chose not to join in taunting the dean.

Her last sentence was repeated in Bob's memory. "Do not take what I say today lightly. In a few years you will have to address the facts just presented to you." Bob feels the need to remain seated. Many of his peers are still booing one minute after she finished and sat down. The dean had a big chance to make a favorable impression on this afternoon. She dropped the ball.

The next speaker to address the graduating class is Dr. John Roberts, President of Central Illinois University. No more than ten seconds into his speech, a graduate pulls out a beach ball. The crowd starts to toss and hit it around, distributing it throughout the arena. Because of the deep Southern accent in his voice, it is difficult to understand everything he is saying. After two minutes of play, an upset faculty member takes the ball. He proceeds to leave with the ball, drawing the anger and boos from the crowd. Many of the graduates shout various obscenities (perhaps they had been drinking before), due to the perceived injustice done by this employee to lessen their amusement.

Once the president finishes his remarks, the main speaker is introduced. "Dr. Who from Where talking about WHAT?" was Bob's response to this individual. He whispered his remark, but his feelings were commonly shared throughout the audience. Perhaps some faculty members know who he is. After all, they are the research experts in their particular fields, but not today's graduates. They have as much clue as Bob does as to who this renowned person is. Despite his credentials, to them he is a nobody. He wasn't some famous celebrity, some of who are asked by 50 or more universities each year to give their commencement address.

After his speech the "calling of the names" began. Bob soon hears the words he has been waiting to hear since his arrival that morning:

"WILL THOSE CANDIDATES FOR GRADUATION WITH A DEGREE OF POLITICAL SCIENCE PLEASE STEP FORWARD TO RECEIVE YOUR DIPLOMAS."

With a certain feeling of pride and relief, Bob stands up and proceeds toward the front stage. In his mind rush many thoughts: 1. The support he received from his family, all of whom are present today, 2. Thousands of hours spent doing research in the library, 3. Writing numerous term papers, 4. Late nights studying outside the laundry room, waiting for his clothes to dry, 5. Countless parties he attended, 6. The night he and Tracy met at the bar, 7. In total, the fun times were coming to an abrupt halt, as his name would soon be announced to 10,000 people.

He felt a great deal of self-respect upon hearing the words ROBERT ANDREW HAMLIN stated over the loudspeaker. Bob gives the presenter of his diploma a firm handshake while accepting his certificate with his free hand. Upon returning to his row, he sees his family cheering. He smiles and waves his hand to accept his brief moment of academic fame and accomplishment. Bob wanted to toss his cap, but quickly reconsiders. "Twenty rows up, no that's too high . . . even for me," Bob states to himself before returning to his seat.

Bob did not always know what he wanted to do, so in that regard he was like most college students. After a great deal of thought, he became more interested in the field of politics. "Government was not the answer to everything, but it is a tool to provide a better future. If the wealthy are organized and see the benefits from participating in the political process, why shouldn't the rest of us try," Bob stated.

"Higher divorce rates, the breakup of the family structure, and parents being forced to work two (perhaps three) jobs to make ends meet, were tearing at the moral core of society," Bob frequently stated, sometimes while bored in a class or two. He felt that the government did not address certain issues in society. With greater family and financial pressures, people were now giving less of their time to charity.

His view had been learned from a previous candidate for Congress who quoted former President John F. Kennedy "one man or woman can make a difference and everyone should try." However, due to a lack of free time (or other pressures), the impact of one person to make a difference was now greater because fewer people are getting involved. Bob's reasoning could appear to the average person to be hypocritical. After all, his sense of charity and civic volunteer work concerned political activities: registering people to vote, discussing issues by going "door-to-door," etc. Nevertheless, he felt the concept was the same as aiding your church or other more meaningful charitable activities. "What cause or need you provide help or money to is not as important as the fact you are helping other people in need." Bob deeply believed. To Bob these were not just opinions: it was a way of life.

Unfortunately, Bob's concern for society often did not fully extend into his private life. However, the air temperature outside resembled the status between Bob and Tracy in their relationship. "Bob always tries to find things to occupy his time. Meeting him to relax and just enjoy my company has become near impossible. Often times, him doing his thing frequently comes at the expense of spending quality time with me!" she declared. She often wondered if he would do it deliberately. "Why does he feel for people so much?

Sometimes. . .I just wish he was like other people and did NOT care," Tracy stated in frustration.

Comparably as Tracy felt about problems in their relationship, Bob had convinced himself that he had learned to deal with problems much better. He believed that he became annoyed less frequently. Boy was he.

Chapter Nine
Learn By Listening, Not Speaking

. . . WRONG!!! For most people it takes a strong realization of the facts or the "hard truth" to admit we are wrong. For Bob, however, such an admission of truth was never really difficult. Like everyone else, he would think he was right. "Bob is as stubborn as anyone," Tracy frequently shouted. When presented with the evidence disproving his viewpoint, on most occasions he would concede on his position. "I make it a point to apologize when I'm wrong. I've never needed to be asked to find someone I hurt. . . I seek them out," Bob painfully seated with a tear when apologizing to Tracy during a previous argument.

Bob made a big mistake in thinking that graduate school would be easy. He was not the smartest person or the best writer, but he had developed some very good study habits. He learned how to budget his time well, a role that was vitally important to someone like Bob who frequently took upon himself too many tasks. He had enjoyed a large amount of academic success thus far. "Why would it not continue in graduate school?" he asked himself. Bob did not fear hard work or burning the midnight oil to complete his class assignments. However, he underestimated the large bulk of reading assignments.

In his first semester, Bob signed up for four courses. Two classes were Graduate Seminars. These "400 level" classes consisted of about eight to twelve students. The assignments in Public Administration and Bureaucracy required a large bulk of readings and a minimum length term paper of 20 pages. They had to be read before each class for discussion between a small core of students and the professor. It was by no means your typical college course. It wasn't a 300-person lecture hall. The class met only one night per week. "Not being ready to discuss the material meant you could be awarded the death sentence," Bob heard a fellow professor say when describing graduate school. For not complying with the established rules set forth by the instructor, your grade could be lowered. "Oh great, one slip-up and there goes the future . . .And some people truly believe grades are unimportant," Bob whispered on the first day of class.

His second seminar was a Research Methods course. The title might lead most people to think that it was intended to show ways of obtaining difficult to find information. However, the course taught you how to perform different analyses of statistics. After inputting the data into a computer, certain relationships could be concluded. In more simple terms, it allowed you to prove some theories or hypotheses by allowing the computer to demonstrate the point you set forth to verify.

Each of Bob Hamlin's four classes was very different. His political philosophy class, however, created the most problems for him. Bob had specialized in "deductive" thinking---coming to an end by using facts, evidence, numbers, etc. In the Socratic Method, answers were determined by using "inductive" reasoning ---the arrival of certain truths by the use of logic. Quite simply, allowing someone to agree with you because of the thoughtfulness of your logic or doing the right thing, and by permitting the learner to discover the weakness of his own opinion without arguing. Using facts, numbers, brute force, etc didn't do it.

The other reason the course was very difficult for Bob was the professor, Dr. Philip Regan. As a man of thought, Bob perceived Dr. Regan to be a genius; someone who would have followed Socrates in 'drinking from the cup' (Socrates' death was induced from drinking cyanide in water. Socrates willingly chose death because he had lived his life preparing for it). But as a professor, Bob felt Dr. Regan was simply a failure. His students did not respect him. It was well known in the department to students and faculty members alike: avoid him.

The class was graded rather differently from most other college courses. Class participation was 40 percent of the weighted grade. In most classes, it is ten percent, if used at all. You simply HAD to come to class. Even if you had an IV in your arm or if you had simply not read the material, your presence was expected. Another student described the class participation part of the grade as follows:

"You ALWAYS came to Regan's class, regardless of the circumstances. You could be in bed with the flu, but you always came. If you were sick, you just 'propped' a stick behind your back against the chair to keep upright. If you were shy or quiet, you learned to nod a lot and you ALWAYS smiled when Dr. Regan did. And comparing a philosophical figure to any religious leader mentioned in the Bible would ALWAYS earn a smile from the professor."

The class did not have a term paper, but a "memoir to offer how the material learned in the class could be used by today's college students" was required. No specific length was ever provided, but a minimum of 30 pages was a good guideline as to where to start. Bob preferred classes where the assignments were clearly provided, deadlines offered, and expectations listed. A conflict between Bob and the professor was inevitable.

"Robert," as Dr. Regan would address him, "what was the deeper meaning to what our focus for today's readings was trying to say?"

Bob then replied, "Do you mean in terms of achieving an alternative path to the truth or by what we should really think the author has stated?" As he spoke, his voice was filled with doubts.

"In terms of your heart Robert. How shall we proceed and address those problems that confront us on a daily basis? What shall be gained from our discussion today?" Dr. Regan asked.

Bob answered the questions by thinking to himself. "What we're trying to do Doc, is receive three credit hours, get an A or B to make our parents happy, and keep the action going until 3:15 p.m. . . . Since I was the winner of today's grand prize by being called upon, let me be truthful. We can forget about applying philosophy to finding the truth for college students. They do not care enough to vote or learn what happens in the world. Quite frankly, they don't care much about anyone but themselves . . . How could they possibly care about a path to the truth. Hope you find the key to the door of having a clue, Dr. Regan."

However, Bob was smart enough not to state out loud what he just thought. Since he had been quiet for a few moments while "thinking", he began by apologizing for not answering the question the right way. He asked his classmates for forgiveness for allowing him to patiently review the question at hand. He stated the discussion reminded him of what he had heard in the homily from the previous

Sunday's Mass at St. Anthony's, the Catholic Church near the campus.

"The question posed to us today is just one path to the truth. Achieving inner peace and respecting our neighbors is a worthy goal and path to pursue. However, there is no one path for ALL of us to follow in finding the truth, for it is not the same for everyone. This may sound strange everyone, but. . ."

Bob is interrupted by Dr. Regan who responds, "There is no sense of being strange in matters close to the heart, Robert," Dr. Regan's voice is heard in the same low tone of a counselor, not the college professor or lecturer.

"If I were to offer to you a way to discover the truth, I would be misguiding you all. The path is not for me or anyone else to offer. It is a way of life we make visible to others by our actions. By the way we act we serve as guideposts, not street signs. I must apologize to you all. . .I will have to respectfully decline to answer what I feel in my heart to be true. I am mature enough in life experiences, but naive in the number of life's circumstances to admit that I may very well be wrong - and serve as an incorrect teacher for you to learn from," Bob states to the other members of the class. The look of innocence on his face is clearly evident.

Dr. Regan is smiling from ear to ear; just as Bob felt would be his response. His classmates have looks of disbelief on their faces because they know that Bob is lying through his teeth in trying to "brown nose" the professor. After all, he missed going to church this past weekend because he was "praying to St. Mattress" by sleeping in. This episode aside, most of the conversations between Bob and Dr. Regan did not proceed as smoothly. The differences between Bob's "live and learn" credo and the professor's "path to the truth" lifestyle just were not compatible. The only real event both looked forward to was the final examination.

The test was 20 percent of the grade. There were no questions to answer and the time limit was thirty minutes. Your "philosophical partner," a classmate and you, were to actively engage in a conversation about whatever the leader chose to discuss. Each student was permitted fifteen minutes to lead and guide the discussion. There was no right or wrong answers, which conflicted with Bob's trained way of learning. However, there was an expected course of how the talk was to go. When the half hour had concluded, Bob and his partner were on the same path - going nowhere fast!! Afterwards Bob was very pleased the course had ended. "I hope Dr. Regan can find the path to the truth or. . .a CAVE that he's looking for!" Bob shouted. He had been asked to describe his "academic adversary." Bob later learned that a perfect attendance score of "A" had salvaged his grade because he had failed the final exam. He earned a "B" for the class.

State Government proceeded much better for all parties involved. The class met twice a week and the grading requirements included a term paper, three exams, some quizzes, and a more responsible class participation grade of 10 percent were more typical of most college classes. Bob felt a better line of communication was clearly present between the two. He believed he was "in like flint" with the professor.

In addition to his problems in the classroom, Bob was having some severe hardships in his personal life. Things between him and Tracy were going downhill really fast. Tracy was most upset because she and Bob were not spending much time together. When they were together, Tracy felt Bob was not really there. His head was always focused on some paper due the next day and it was beginning to tear at the core of their relationship. A typical evening's talk would go something like this:

"Tracy, here we go again. How many times do we have to go through this? We have discussed this topic at least twenty times now. Between my work and class assignments, I have NO more free time. I have been in the library the previous four hours."

"As for being tired when I get here, I am sorry. I have been running non-stop for the last fourteen hours and I AM tired. It is now 11:00 at night. Well, low and behold, did it ever enter your mind that perhaps I act as if I am tired because I AM tired? It's been a long day and" Bob states as he is interrupted by her.

"Long day again? You know what, it has been a long day for me too. You act as if YOU are the only one who is tired, the only one who is having problems with school, the only PERSON! You have been here fifteen minutes now and you have not even asked how I am doing," Tracy says. At this time she moves next to Bob. Doing so will better position her to imitate Bob. What soon follows is not a very happy sight for either of the two involved. Her speech comes right from the heart and tries to address her greatest concerns with Robert Hamlin. She then pretends to imitate a "potential" discussion between Bob and herself out loud. By potential, Tracy felt more hopeful that it could occur; much like they had conversed with they began dating.

"Hello Tracy. How are you today?" Bob states as he leans forward to give his girlfriend a hug.

"Fine Bob, how are you?" Tracy states in response to Bob's loving display of concern.

"I am doing great," Tracy states as she smiles. The sign of her happiness is very clear with the expression on her face.

They are still in a firm embrace when he replies, "My day went very well, but please tell me how your day was," Bob states to her.

"Thanks for asking Bob. YOU really do take great interest in my life. I am SO LUCKY to have a boyfriend like you," Tracy says with a large smile, which suddenly changes into a look of anger! Her act of their "conversation" was a clear signal to him of how she really felt. There was little room to misjudge her true feelings about their relationship at the present time. Tracy sits down on the couch, seething with anger.

Bob just stands there for a few moments. Three minutes later, Bob sits down and joins her on the couch, keeping a distance between them of a few feet. If he says the wrong thing, he does not want to be slapped. He would much prefer to give her a hug to let her know he loves her. However, after dating Tracy for over a year now, he is smart enough to recognize that she is very angry with him.

After sorting in his mind what should be said, he responds. "I know you are right. You do not have to persuade me that I have not been the greatest company for you recently. I know that sometimes I act as if my head is elsewhere when I am with you. I am very sorry, but I have been very busy this semester. That does not mean you have not been busy either. Sometimes I wonder how I have been sleeping well with all the stress and number of deadlines I have been under."

"I know you would rather get together under better circumstances. We both deserve to enjoy the pleasure of each other's company. But based on both of our work and school schedules, it is very difficult right now. Perhaps we should both be a little more aware of the present situation and just calm down. This semester I have been 'burning the candle' at three ends. I did not expect graduate school would be this hard with four to six deadlines per week. Believe me Tracy, I wish that things were going better for both of us in school and in our relationship.

"I am a VERY lucky guy to have the chance to date you. Do not think I don't know that. Oh, I almost forgot, I have something for you," Bob declares. He gets up and goes across the room to obtain his school bag. In addition to his numerous folders, photocopied pages, and class notes, is a red rose. He withdraws the flower and returns to Tracy on the couch.

"I just wanted you to know that I love you. Despite all of our current problems we are having now, it does not change how I feel about you," Bob states. He and Tracy smile and embrace in a long hug.

"You know, deep down beneath your firm handshake and cute smile is someone who cares more about other people than himself … I love you," Tracy says. After a periodic laugh, they then begin to chat and enjoy the pleasure of each other's company without any regard to time, deadlines, or outside interferences. The only break the two have is for an occasional kiss.

Bob is startled as he wakes up again. It is 3:10 in the morning and he discovers he is full of sweat. "Here it is only in April and it is hot as hell in here. What will it be like in July." He is very much surprised from the events over the past few hours. "You know, I always sleep better after I have had some water," Bob whispers. He then gets up and proceeds toward the bathroom. Drinking two full cups of water, he returns to his bedroom. Bob thinks about what has happened in his sleep, occasionally shaking with anxiety. He then states:

"There must be an easier way than this. Never before in my life have I given ANY thought to my future or what I wanted to do. From what I have seen tonight, there is some level of hope for me. My life, as shown, does have goals and organization. Hell, in my dreams I even have a college major, a degree and a method to get things done, on time. But Political Science? How and why the hell did I come up with that? I don't even know the name of my Congressman" Bob says. His voice is filled with disgust as he pulls the sheets over his head.

Tracy and he exchange a long hug at the door, her face filled with sadness.

"What's wrong Tracy?" Bob asks.

"Just sad to see you go . . . But I am glad we talked tonight. I will call you in twenty minutes to make sure you got home okay," Tracy says as they kiss good-bye.

Bob departs the building and begins his long climb up the hill toward his door. "I really like visiting Tracy, but I hate this damn walk," Bob declares as he kicks a rock down the street just like a soccer player would hit a ball with his foot.

The following day is his least favorite, Tuesday. Bob's schedule consists of a State Government class in the morning followed by working office hours for a professor. Lunch with a few friends is at Noon; "fun with philosophy" begins at two in the afternoon and then dinner. His evening consists of a seminar on Public Administration for three hours. Each student is expected to fully participate in class discussion. Just "showing up" or not falling asleep will not be acceptable. Bob had concluded that NO class is worthy of a three-hour length of time.

The professor is a noted expert in the field, Dr. Joyce Hyland. Her 900-page doctoral thesis revealed two things to Bob: An ability to talk, a lot, about a very serious subject, and an abundance of research done on a subject not well known to most citizens.

"Nine hundred pages? Most people do not produce or write that much paperwork in their entire lives. . . let alone on one major school assignment," Bob says while thinking to himself. "One can only imagine the MINIMUM length of this term paper. Nine hundred pages! Give me a break," Bob repeats.

"Upon review of your syllabus you will notice that the length of YOUR term paper is only 20 to 25 pages," Dr. Hyland states while describing her 'vision' of her students' work products. A syllabus is a listing of all assignments due for a college class. It gives due dates of papers, when tests are, and lists other important rules and requirements of the class.

"But what is NOT prevalent here is length. I want your papers to 'shine like the sun on a hot summer day.' The length of the sun's presence is limited, but the heat and generated energy are very warm. Go ahead and make me very proud," Dr. Hyland declares with her arms extended upward to the ten students present.

The syllabus in this class met all of Bob's requirements for being good. It itself was nine pages in length. It included what was to be read, what was to be discussed on what nights and when the major exams were. "A good syllabus is the best way to minimize differences between the professor and the students," Bob declared with a smile. "Particularly when having detail-oriented people like myself." In most instances a question in assignments or grading would be of the student's error. Regardless of its importance, most students only read it during the first week of the semester, relying on the professor for what will be due when. In every class, there is one student who tries to "test" the patience of the professor by challenging the established rules of the game. It's not that Bob liked being the guinea pig. "Let's just keep it. . .simple," Bob stated.

He did the best he could in graduate school, but was not a candidate for a Rhodes scholarship, the prestigious award that permits American college students to study abroad in England. However, his grades were good enough to keep his assistantship. What kept him going, particularly when times were very difficult was the view that Bob's next semester would be much easier. He would not have ten term papers to write, perhaps only five or six. The pressure he and other graduate students faced would be severely reduced and he was hoping he could enjoy school again and spend more time with Tracy. Bob frequently reminded himself. "If I finish this semester I'm home free. I'd have rounded third base and would be headed home for the winning run."

When the final exams ended, his grades came just before Christmas. He soon realized that the hardest three and a half months of his life were over. Bob was looking forward to being able to relax and enjoy the following four weeks over the holiday break. In a remarkable twist of fate and luck, his life was forever changed on Saturday, December 19th. On this day, he walked into a convenience store located just two blocks away from his home. Things would never be the same.

Chapter Ten
Winning the Game

As Bob was making a break for the door he heard a familiar voice ring out from down the hall. "Oh Bob," Mrs. Hamlin yelled out. "Are you going somewhere?"

"Oops," Bob responded. Bob was hoping that he could slip out the door unnoticed. He was not opposed to helping his family. He had always assisted with little chores around the home. He just felt hard pressed on this occasion because he was running ten minutes late. It was the Saturday before Christmas and Bob was due to go shopping with Tracy after picking her up. She lived in a town called Downers Grove, a suburb located to the west of Chicago.

"Could you please run an errand for me? We've run out of bread and milk. Whoever had 'em last did not leave a note. It's almost dinner time and your help would. . ." Mrs. Hamlin stated. She was preparing dinner for the family.

"Sure thing. Don't worry, I'll go for you," Bob answers. While walking back into the kitchen, he mumbles to himself, "It can't be too bad. After all, I have to get a newspaper anyway."

His mother gives him three dollars to cover the price of the two items she needs. "Thanks. I really appreciate your help," Mrs. Hamlin states with a smile to her eldest son. The convenience store was a frequent stop for members of the Hamlin family if they needed a few grocery items.

After arriving at the store, he repeats his shopping list. "I need a newspaper, a gallon of milk, and a loaf of bread," Bob whispers when exiting the car. While standing in the check out line, he notices the ad for the state's lottery. "Tonight's Lotto, worth $12 million." Bob debates buying a ticket for a moment, then concludes "$12 million dollars. I could sure use that money. Hell, it only costs a dollar," Bob states in a happy tone. He is easily impressed by little things and "besides, it's Christmas time."

He purchases these items and approaches the counter to where the line for the lottery is located. There's already a crowd; including twelve rainbow chasers. Bob stands at the end of the line waiting for his turn to buy a ticket. He enjoys the thrill of what could happen if he won, but he is also smart enough to know the odds of winning the game. "While taking a calculus class in college, I learned the odds of winning the grand prize were nearly 13 million to 1. And contrary to what most people think, the odds of winning do not double when you buy twice as many tickets," Bob thought to himself. Many times in the past he had seen some 'clown' spending $40 to win the Lotto. Bob would see someone like that and say "What a waste. Another graduate of our failed education system. . . A fool who believes that betting his weekly cigarette money will make him rich forever."

Despite these facts and the long odds, the two people ahead of Bob are serious players. One just bought $20 worth of tickets. When his son asked if he could have a candy bar, the father replied, "No, we do not have any money today." His tone was rude, prompting his son to cry. The other person in line is chain-smoking cigarettes, in clear violation of the NO SMOKING sign. He hands the clerk a set of pre-selected numbers, indicating he is a frequent player. "Okay sir. That will be $45," an employee by the name of "Betty" tells the customer.

Bob notices the man has some difficulty paying the clerk because he is choking. "Perhaps if you would handle one task at a time, you would have an easier time," Bob states to himself. While still coughing, he is fumbling his hands between the money, the tickets, and a pack of cigarettes. Bob now has been in the store for fifteen minutes and is really running late.

"It is simply amazing how you can fool the people in the state of Illinois. Just create a game, tell 'em the money is for education, and watch the players run to play" Bob mumbles to himself. He then sighs deeply to help alleviate the tension that has been built up by waiting in line. "One dollar on Quick Pick in tonight's Lotto game please," Bob clearly says. "After all, I have the same chance as some idiot who buys $40 worth of tickets," he states out loud. The man who had purchased the game tickets ahead of him turns around toward Bob, coughing violently and wondering what he meant.

After buying his ticket he leaves the store with the other items he bought for his mom. Since he is now running almost an hour late, he decides to call Tracy. He puts the grocery items down on the kitchen table. After dialing the number he gets an invention made famous: the answering machine.

"Hi, it's me. I am running very late now because I ran an errand for my Mom. I'm leaving now. I love you. Bye," Bob says as he hangs up. He says goodbye to his Mother and leaves their house.

After arriving at Tracy's home they proceed to the mall. She likes the small items that are on sale.

She even tells Bob, "Look, this is on sale for fifty percent off. I am saving money."

But Bob soon replies, "Yea, you just spent nearly $50 saving us money."

Despite having differences over money, as most couples do, they really do enjoy each other's company shopping for holiday gifts. The next half hour Bob describes how people walk into each other without concern for anyone but themselves. "And to think, it's Christmas. Time to share with others who are not as fortunate. Yep, care and concern for one another," Bob says jokingly, repeating a phrase he heard each day while attending his Catholic grammar school. They decide to rent a movie and return to her house.

"Happy holidays, Scrooge," Tracy says as both she and Bob laugh at Bob's lack of the Christmas spirit.

"Thanks for brining me back to Earth. . .Everyday I'm with you, I realize how good you are to me and how lucky I am. Merry Christmas," Bob says as they kiss each other.

Around midnight, Bob arrives back at home. While entering his bedroom, Bob says in a real somber tone, "It's been a long day. Low and behold, I am going to bed." After removing his clothes, he soon falls asleep.

The following morning he goes downstairs to perform one of his favorite activities: reading the Sunday papers. He reads EVERYTHING, not just the sports or cover stories. Bob remembers he had purchased a lottery ticket the evening before so he returns to his room to get it.

Still rubbing his eyes to remove the crust that formed the night before, he sits down at the table. He then compares the numbers on his ticket to those listed in the paper. While reading them he sees a pattern developing between the two sets. While checking his ticket, he observes that his numbers match those listed as the winning numbers from the night before. He cannot believe his eyes as he shakes with excitement.

"Hold on, let me check this," Bob whispers with his voice shaking with fear. "Eight, 8; 12,12; 34, 34; 39, 39; I WON, I WON, I WON! HEY EVERYONE, I WON! EVERYONE COME HERE QUICK. . . I WON!" Bob shouts at the top of his lungs. He is running around the house looking for anyone to tell the good news to.

Since it was early Sunday morning, some members of the Hamlin family were still sleeping. However, his mom enters the kitchen and finds Bob there. He is jumping up and down and is breathing heavy. After all, he has run around the house twice already.

"Bob, WHAT ARE YOU YELLING ABOUT? It's Sunday," Mrs. Hamlin asks after lowering her voice.

"I won the lottery. See, just look here. I have the winner!!!" Bob responds. He is nearly panting with excitement. Even the family dog is happy. Buster jumps onto Bob and begins licking his face. Bob does not even care about the dog's actions because he is so thrilled by the news. After all, he can now afford to buy lots of dogs.

"OH MY GOD!!. . .COME HERE. YOUR SON HAS WON!! YOU WILL NOT BELIEVE THIS!!! Bob where are you?" Mrs. Hamlin shouts. She then turns toward her son to give him a hug.

"What's all the noise about? Why's everyone yelling? What's wrong now? Did you lose your money or some clothes again to the house thief?" Mr. Hamlin questions. Bob has complained on numerous occasions how some of his personal possessions have disappeared over the years.

"You won't believe this. He's has won the lottery! Look here. Check it out!" Mrs. Hamlin responds. She is almost as excited as Bob, who by this time is jumping up and down in the front yard.

"Okay, let's take a look at what's making you create this . . . racket. Don't want you making TOO MUCH noise for nothing," Mr. Hamlin speaks. He is completely unaware of the validity of Bob's winning ticket.

"8, 8; 12,12; 28, 28; 34,34; 39, 39; 43,43. You really won!!! What a miracle!!! By the way, where'd he go?" Mr. Hamlin says.

The two of them proceed to the front door. Bob. He is leaping up and down like a pogo stick. Everyone in the Hamlin family has always viewed him to be a little different from everyone else, particularly themselves. Despite some of the strange things he says, his parents are very happy for him, even if he is making a complete fool of himself.

"I WON, I WON, I WOONNN!!" Bob shouts as he returns toward the house. He now has calmed down to the point of being able to walk straight. "By the way has anyone seen the ticket?" Bob asks.

His mom then returns his ticket and passport of personal wealth back to him.

"Glad you're paying attention…you know me…I'd lose my head if it wasn't attached…thanks! I need to call Tracy so I can tell her the news." He goes upstairs to put the ticket away in a safe place. After all, he will need to find it later.

He picks up the phone and calls his girlfriend. The phone rings three times and Bob is soon becoming impatient. "Come on. . . don't give me the (answering) machine, pick up the phone," Bob says with a grunt.

"Hello," a female answers.

"Hi, it's me," Bob states.

"Oh hi. How are you?" she asks.

"I'm doing great. Got some fantastic news for you, well, I mean, us. I. . ." Bob declares as Tracy interrupts him.

"Hey, I'm really sorry, but I have to interrupt you. My family is walking out the door to go to church. We're running late," Tracy answers.

"Well call the church and tell them to delay the service. I JUST WON THE LOTTERY," Bob responds in a very clear voice. There was no chance she could misinterpret what he said. Bob hears silence at the other end, so he proceeds to repeat what he stated. "I WON THE LOTTERY!"

"You did what? How? I mean. . . How do you know?" Tracy answers him while stuttering.

"Just checked the numbers and mine matched all of those in the paper. Unless there's a mistake, I am a very wealthy man," Bob replies in an elevated voice. "Did you hear me, I won!" he asserts.

"You won? Yeaaaaaa!! All right! We're happy for you. I mean, I'm happy for us . . . Got to get going, for they're signaling for me to go," Tracy states. Her level of happiness is increasing by the minute.

"Don't worry about being late now. With the money I just won, we can BUY a church. We can set a schedule and Sunday services at OUR convenience," Bob replies while laughing at the prospect.

"That's not funny at all," Tracy states, clearly showing her disapproval with his statement.

"Look I know. I'm just teasing you. Go with your family to church. I NEED to get some things done here. . . like confirm the winning numbers. Probably need to speak with a lawyer soon. Buy yourself a nice dress Trace. We'll have a ceremony to attend this week. We'll talk later. Give me a call when you return home," Bob speaks.

"Congratulations hon, we're very happy for you, I mean us," Tracy declares, already picturing herself, as most people would do, with a share of the money. She and Bob are doing better in their relationship but aren't yet engaged yet. Nor has the topic really been discussed between them in their relationship. Later, she felt more comfortable when she remembered how Bob stated "I have great news for us" in their hurried discussion.

Hanging up the phone, Bob starts to look for the number to call for the lottery headquarters. Later, because of frustration, he decides to call a local radio station. He looks up the number to WNEW, an all-news radio station in Chicago. After being transferred two or three times, he finally was able to speak with someone in the newsroom.

"Yes, can you please provide me with last night's winning numbers in the lotto game?" Bob asks of the newsroom attendant.

"Okay, that's good. And how much was the game for! Twelve million dollars, fine. . . Oh, one last question, could you check to see how many winning tickets were sold. . . Two winners. Good. . . real good. Thanks for your help today," Bob says

"Why do you want to know so much?" the female employee asks.

"Well, my name is Bob and I purchased one of the two winning tickets. Just wanted to confirm the numbers. . . My last name? You'll have to wait until next week. . . Am I dating anyone? HA-HA-HA-HA-HA. Thank you," Bob shouts, still laughing as he hangs up the phone from the question posed to him.

Bob then decides to call a friend of his who he knows from some political activities who is an attorney. After dialing the number, Jim answers the call at the other end.

"Hello," Jim states.

"Jim, how you doing today. This is Robert Hamlin. I'm really sorry to call you on a Sunday morning, but I need to ask you something. Is there a chance that you and I could sit down to talk today?" Bob asks.

"Well, yea. For how long? Is there something wrong? Do you need help?" his friend Jim questions in response. After all, he has no idea why Bob has called.

"No, no nothing is wrong. Actually something is very RIGHT because I just received some good news. However, I'll need to speak to someone about a legal issue. Since you are an attorney, you immediately came to mind. It should take no more than one hour. Since its Sunday, I'll do my best to limit our time . . . But I still think it would be best to talk ASAP before. . . Can we talk today?" Bob asks with a strong sense of urgency in his voice.

"Is 3:00 okay with you?" Jim asks, wondering what Bob has on his mind.

"Perfect. We can keep it very brief. . . By the way, thanks again for meeting with me on a Sunday afternoon. Most people would not. . . Thanks a lot," Bob states as he hangs up the telephone. Jim is confused after he puts down the receiver. After all, he still has NO IDEA what the meeting is about.

Later in the afternoon, Bob is walking out the door. He departs his parents' home around 2:40 p.m. to travel to Flossmoor, a suburb about five miles away from the Hamlin residence in Park Forest, where Jim lives with his family. At 2:55 p.m. Bob arrives at Jim's house and approaches the front door. "One of my biggest pet peeves is people who are late. I mean. . . they're never on time. That's why I'm here now," Bob says. Since he greatly appreciated Jim's willingness to give up some free time on a Sunday afternoon, which Bob referred to as family day, he made an extra effort to be on time. "Being punctual is an easy way to show you care," Bob whispers while ringing the doorbell.

"How are you?" Jim asks as he gives Bob a warm greeting with a firm handshake. "Come in and make yourself comfortable. Is there anything we can get for you to drink?" Jim asks his lucky guest.

"A glass of water will be fine. It helps me think straight," Bob replies. Jim's wife Barbara goes into the kitchen and fills up a large pitcher of water. Bob and her husband continue to exchange greetings in the other room.

Despite Bob's enthusiasm earlier today, Jim observes that he is very quiet today. "Thank you," Bob states as he is handed a cup of water. After a few minutes Jim decides to 'break the ice' as to why Bob has requested such a meeting on short notice.

"So... it's such a nice day outside. What would prompt you to ask for a meeting on this Sunday afternoon?" Jim inquires of his political associate and friend.

"Today I discovered how great life can really be. Lady Luck likes me. I matched all six numbers to win the grand prize in the (Illinois) lotto game," Bob says.

"That's wonderful news. Congratulations," Jim replies.

"After going nuts from the news, I literally woke up my entire family. To confirm the news, I called the radio station. After all, you would not want me bothering you if I did not really win, right? An employee verified for me the six numbers needed to win from last night's game. She even told me that the state had announced there were two winners. The winning pool was drawn from a total of $12 million," Bob stated.

"Wow. Fantastic. I'm very happy for you and your family. . . But why are you calling me with the news?" Jim asked.

"Well, I need some help and will probably need some legal advice. I have done some thinking today about my future. Do you think I should finish school, travel or form a business? As you know, I love politics. I really think that I'd be a good political consultant. Should

I buy a house?. . . I guess I have a lot of questions. What should I do?" Bob asks of his friend. He wanted to question someone for advice who was not in his family.

"The best answer is probably your least favorite. Staying in school and finishing college. You're in grad school, right? This will allow you to finish what you've started. After all, you've completed a semester, correct?" Jim questions.

Bob nods his head in approval.

"Okay then, finish the program. Get the advanced degree. Sure, you'll have the money now, but you never know what the future holds. No one likes a quitter. When you get married and start having children, your energy level or simply your commitment to finish school won't be there. But now, your free time IS available. You have your whole life to travel and enjoy yourself...Finish school first. Later on, you may want to consider going to law school. The main problem in the past for you was money, right?"

Bob nods in approval again. "Plus, my LSAT (Law School Admissions Test) score was low. My roommate was up all night drunk. Didn't get any sleep," Bob replies with a laugh.

"That happens in college. That time period also known as the best five or six years of one's life. But for you, if you want to run for (public) office sometime (Bob and Jim first met by working on the same political campaign) taking the time now may prove to be very helpful. It'll allow you the chance to show to other people that you can be responsible with your money. . .That you can finish what you started. If you go out and waste the money spoiling yourself, most people would not view such actions positively, especially people older than you. I've known you for a while. You're a good person and I'm sure you'll do the right thing," Jim declares.

What I'm saying is this: using the money you have won to get the best education you can, painful and boring as it may sound, may prove better than some stock dividend return or large investment," Jim states.

During the entire time he spoke, Bob did not interrupt once. "I've had a bad habit of not listening," Bob admitted to some close friends. But I've been working hard to overcome this weakness." Bob states.

"And before you ask about buying a home, just ask yourself this: If you were to purchase a home, would you move in it right away? Remember you would have to maintain it, cook meals for yourself all while you are away at school. You can't be at two places at the same time. If you choose to remain in school, it probably would be hard living in your new home AND attending classes."

"Hey, thanks for reading my mind," Bob replies.

"My simple advice is this: complete school. Once that's done, if you want to buy a house or go to law school or. . .just to have a place to live, that's fine. But don't rush into anything too fast... besides, you may be forgetting a key fact still," Jim declares.

"What's that?" Bob inquires with a puzzled look on his face.

"You haven't received your first check yet," Jim states in a firm voice, as they both begin to laugh.

"You make a lot of sense. It may not be what I want to hear, but you're right. But...there's another reason I am here today. As you know, I'll need an attorney to prepare some legal documents and to represent me. I have some ideas as to how I would like to spend the money. Could you help me?" Bob requests of Jim, who is both a close friend and infrequent political advisor. A smile was developing on Bob's face, as if he already knew what the answer would be.

"I'd be honored to Bob. Let me get a legal pad. It will allow me to take some notes. This way we can begin the process to put onto paper what you'd like to do. After all, it is your money," Jim declares. He appreciates Bob's offer to represent him, but Jim wants to make sure that Bob knows who was responsible for their being together today.

Jim leaves the room. Upon obtaining all the necessary materials, he returns to the dining room where the two had been talking.

"Okay, I think were ready now. Tell me what you want to do. You have won a pot of gold without seeking the rainbow. Roll the bones," Jim states in an upbeat tone.

"I want to help people, but I don't have the ego to need to be begged for the money. Remember when Jim Harbaugh (an NFL quarterback who was formerly with the Chicago Bears) announced he was going to give his salary to charity until the Bears won. All those groups faxed him requests of how they needed it... It was as if they saw a gold mine and they came running for it…it was pathetic. They looked like vultures."

"What I want to do is give the money to some worthy charities without the public circus. I'd like to limit my donations to some different charities, each receiving about $5,000 per year. They are as follows: 1. American Cancer Society, 2. American Lung Association, 3. United Negro College Fund, 4. Black Lung Disease (a common disease of coal miners), 5. AIDS research, 6. Breast Cancer Research, and 7. Central Illinois University. Oh, I'd also like to help my church. I want each to receive a letter with the check to clearly indicate that this is a donation to a good cause. All of these groups can spend the money any way they wish, with no strings attached."

"However the school I attend must spend the money recruiting better basketball players from the Chicago area. The only thing these college sports programs understand is money anyway. I've written multiple letters offering my advice. . .It's a damn shame the system revolves around money. Perhaps I'll have the ear of the athletic department now," Bob says. Jim was smiling, but Bob wasn't, trying to show how serious he was. "As a matter of fact, I'd consider giving even more to my alumnus if they are successful at what they have been assigned. If not, their money can be revoked to help a better goal and effort. After all, the need is great in America despite our nation being very wealthy."

"Also, I'd like to set up a yearly scholarship trust fund. Ten winners per year for a $1,000 prize to America's college students. They must write an essay about what would they do to improve America if they win the lottery? Ask them to picture themselves winning $6 million to be paid over twenty years. I want to see what other young people would do. There are so many areas of need. As you know older Americans view my age group as the LOST GENERATION, a couple million nobodies who don't care about anyone but themselves. I'm out to change that. We should each be judged as individuals, regardless of how many birthday candles we have on the cake."

"I'm now in the position to help others now. I really enjoy doing so. I also understand the responsibility of what it means to be in this financial position. Most often, poor or disadvantaged people lack the political or financial clout to lobby our government officials. Many lack the knowledge to know where to go to ask for and receive the help they need. Believe me, this does not mean anyone is stupid. To get help, one must know where to turn. Were all human beings and deserve respect."

"I called you today to help me prepare these documents. I'd like this to be ready when my family and I, accompanied by you, go before the public to announce that we've won. How does one week from this Wednesday sound for you?" Bob asks.

"Wow, I really do not know what to say. You're what…22? But, you've shown a great deal of maturity with the vision to help some good causes. Most of us, however, may wonder as to how and why those particular charities were chosen. Or better yet, why the list is exclusive? People will want to know why others cannot or should not apply," Jim stated.

"I'm only mentioning this because you will get some questions on this issue. Your donations represent some…$40,000 to $80,000 per year. Here is something to consider. You might say something like. . . it's your money and you have decided to spend it on a limited number of charities. Their success comes from being able to minimize administrative costs. Time has shown their resources have best gone to help find a cure or provide the help to the greatest number of people," Jim says as he puts down the legal pad. Bob, on a more serious note, are there any other special requirements you'd like to make… such as who would be your beneficiaries?" Jim inquires. He feels bad even bringing up the subject.

"Yea… I know it's hard to ask. I'd like half to go to my parents, one quarter to my girlfriend, and one quarter to the rest of my siblings. When I get married, I'd like the percentages between my parents and my wife to be reversed. Should my parents and I die, divide the money between my wife and my remaining family members, including my siblings, in an 80/20 split.

"Since none of that applies, make the checks payable to me. When all the paperwork is prepared, I'll write you a check for

$5,000, pending it is done right," Bob states with a big smile on his face.

"Well, thanks for calling me today. You know, your generosity is rare. It's a welcome change. I'm glad someone like you won. Anything else I can do?" Jim asks.

"No, that's alright for now. Hey, I just wanted one last time to thank you for the time you gave me today. It's a nice day and there are a whole lot of things we'd rather be doing. Your help does mean a lot to me. . . I almost forgot there's one last thing. My family may ask as to who's getting what and how much. If this happens, could you say something like the details have been noted in a legal trust? I'm not at the liberty to answer any questions about it," Bob answers as Jim nods his head indicating he understands Bob's request for privacy.

Both he and Jim get up to shake hands and exchange their goodbyes. "Please thank your family for their patience and time today," Bob states. "I really appreciate your help."

After a productive afternoon, Bob returns home for dinner with his family. The news of Bob's good luck has spread throughout the household. Everyone who has called the house, whether they know Bob or not, now knows what has happened. It did not take long for his lucky streak to be the main topic of discussion when he walked into the house. He had not even taken his shoes off upon being treated as an American hero in their household.

"Hey Bob! How is my favorite millionaire doing today?" Mrs. Hamlin questions.

"I'm your eldest son, rich or poor, and thanks for asking. I'm doing great," Bob replies with a courteous smile on his face.

"Have you given any thought as to what you are going to do with the money you've won?" Mr. Hamlin, his father, asks.

"No, I haven't given any thought to it. But when I do, you'll be the first to know. However, I would like to help my family financially. Maybe help some charities. Perhaps finish school and then start a business. . . maybe. . . well, other than that, no I haven't decided what to do with the money," Bob answers in response.

"Help out the family and aid a charity, WAY TO GO SON!" Mr. Hamlin shouts after hearing the good news. To add emphasis to his feelings, he raised his fist high into the air and pats Bob on the back. In the past, they had jokingly discussed what they would do if either had won the lottery. Mr. Hamlin now recalls how Bob previously mentioned that he would allow his father to retire if he won.

Questions pertaining to what Bob would do with the money continue later in the day. As the Hamlin family sits down for dinner, thoughts of financial gain jump through their minds. On most occasions, members of the Hamlin family are not always present for dinner. Whether they are away at school or preoccupied with their individual needs or interests they seem to have a hard time getting together to eat as a family. However, on this day they ALL feel their financial picture has changed. Everyone made a point to be present tonight.

His sister Sheila offers where the conversation is headed. She is the most vocal child in the Hamlin household. She is two years younger than Bob. A college sophomore, she's studying to be a teacher at a private university just down the street from where Bob attends school. Although it is his sister's comments, the words could have come from any sibling present tonight.

"Hey everyone, I was talking to my girlfriend Patty today. We were kind of discussing vacation spots. After going back and forth, we settled on going to Acapulco in three weeks. Do you think that would be okay? I mean. . . traveling is soooooo much fun. How does that sound?" Sheila asks. She has a large smile on her face.

Bob has a grin on his face too. "That's wonderful," he states while putting his fork back down on the table. He tries not to be a slob, but you can always tell where he sits at the dinner table. Leaving a mess on his place setting and sharing his meal with the dog have become common during supper. "How are you and your friend going to pay for this trip you have already planned?" Bob naively asks his sister.

"Well. . . we were kind of hoping you could help us out? I mean, it would really be nice to travel, wouldn't it?" she asks.

"Ohhh, I'm sure it would be. However, you may have a slight problem with the funding mechanism. The first check may not come for two to three months, not weeks. The other problem you have is one of courtesy. It appears that you may have gone out spending other people's money. That's kind of rude... before asking for such help.

Bob pauses and takes a few deep breaths before continuing. Much to his family's surprise, he is calm and not in the least bit upset. "My intention of aiding our family is to be of decrease financial burdens, pay off the mortgage, reduce our student loans, etc. I don't plan to sit on a beach drinking pina coladas or wasting the money. If anyone here expects us to 'roll over and play dead' or act as if the money we won is a slush fund or tan enhancer, they are sadly mistaken. Those who have money, whether earned or awarded to them, have a responsibility to be good citizens. But more importantly, to be a living example of how one person shall live and obey the rules in our society.

"Our financial problems may have now ended today, but it does not mean that the free ride is about to begin!" Bob shouts in a renewed sense of anger while pounding the table. He's decided not to hide his emotions anymore. For a brief moment he let his anger get the better of him. However, he clenched his fist tightly to regain his composure. He deliberately waited (and his family remained quiet) until the tone of his voice returned to normal. When it had, Bob resumed speaking.

"Don't you see, as wealthy Americans we now have a responsibility to other people, particularly those not as lucky as us. Not everyone is as fortunate as we are now. It does not mean tossing a quarter to the homeless on the street. But, more importantly, giving money AND our time to established and legitimate groups who provide help to the most vulnerable in our society.

"If we don't get involved when the need is greatest and choose only to entertain ourselves, we're no better than the insider traders and corporate pirates who rob good people of their dignity and their money as they approach their retirement years. . .We're a family. If you want help, I'm here for each and every one of you. But, if you want the money just to impress others while satisfying yourselves, then there's the door...Don't let it hit you on the way out," Bob conveys in a firm but clear voice to the entire family.

After that exchange, the conversation's tone became rather subdued. Perhaps Bob's other siblings had plans themselves, but felt this was not the right time to bring up their ideas. His parents, Mr. and Mrs. Hamlin, sit back in astonishment. Now holding hands, they are never more proud. "Maybe we had dreams of nice vacations. However, after hearing our son speak we should be happy because we are reminded, once again, how we've raised a responsible and mature person as our eldest child," Mrs. Hamlin thinks to herself. "The satisfaction of having a son who cares about other people more than himself is more important than a one week vacation to some far away place."

"Besides, there is no time for individual tanning junkets. We're all going to Florida again as a FAMILY real soon. By the way, everyone can bring a few guests . . . I'm bringing a few myself," Bob declares to the surprised yet happy members of the Hamlin clan, who all begin to cheer in happiness and give each other high-fives. "I was hoping to keep it a surprise, but it just. . ."

Chapter Eleven
Money to Finance the Future

". . . Did not work out. Regardless of how hard I try, I have a hard time keeping a secret. Not telling my girlfriend what I purchased for her at Christmas time is near impossible. I am sure, however, that over time things will improve for me on this matter," Bob states to the members of the media and invited guests present. He and the other winner of the $12 million have come forward today to have their picture taken and prepare the necessary paperwork to receive their first installment payment. Each will earn almost $300,000 per year for twenty years.

"Mr. Hamlin, how do you intend to spend the money?" a reporter from the Chicago Post asks.

"Mr. Hamlin. Please. . . My name is Bob," he replies to the statement with a smile as those present begin to laugh. "I have made arrangements to donate a large amount of money to some different charities each year. In addition, a scholarship fund has been created to provoke some discussion among our young people into answering a question we should all consider as we gather here today: How would they help others if they won the lottery?" Bob states.

"I still am enrolled in graduate school. That should take one more year of my time. Afterwards I hope to go to law school. Most importantly, I want to help my family financially. By winning the lottery, the state of Illinois has been very generous to me. I am willing to accept the responsibility of helping other people. Last of all, I am going to TRY to encourage my parents to retire. Perhaps it will not be easy (Bob glances toward his parents who are standing behind him and smiles), but at least I will try," Bob affirms to all those present.

"Bob, are you married? With your new wealth, you should expect to be approached by many people now" another reporter from the Northtown Express declares.

"Well, anyone who is in my financial position could expect that. However, the only people I would associate myself with, particularly date, are those people who value me as a person. After all, any fool can become wealthy, Bob says as several people begin to laugh. "Each day presents for me a new chance to learn how to become a better person myself."

"I am dating a beautiful young person named Tracy who is here with us today." Tracy smiles before the camera, but turns red from embarrassment. Like anyone else, I expect the offers, but I really have other priorities in my life," Bob replies in a calm manner. The question might have been awkward for most people to answer, especially in the presence of members of his family. "Don't worry. I'm very comfortable answering questions that pertain to my personal life. I've heard and seen it all," Bob replies with a smile. At this point, he has no idea how that specific character trait will help him later in life.

"Are there any other questions today?" Bob inquires of the media representatives present.

After a brief pause one reporter asks, "Yes Bob, since you won the game, are there any regrets or fears you may have?" a member of a local TV station asks.

"Yes. My only regret is that I did not win sooner," Bob responds with a smile.

All present in the room begin to laugh, perhaps surprised by Bob's sense of humor. After all, he has spent the previous twenty minutes being very serious about charitable donations and candid in answering various types of questions that were asked.

"What I mean is that I had a dream a long time ago that I had won the lotto game. After all the previous Saturdays without winning, I was asking myself when this would happen," Bob asserts with a smile. "Hell, I'll be honest, I gave up on winning."

"As for any regrets, no. Everyone I have come across the past two weeks has been very supportive and kind. There have been some odd offers (for sexual favors) and requests for help. They range from needing money to pay the medical bills of dying parents or this and that problem. However, part of winning requires being mature enough to handle such requests. . . Most people have been very understanding since they learned I had won the game. However, if you have any special needs today, feel free to speak with my attorney Jim."

"Having money is very tempting for any human being. It allows you the financial luxury to try different things. I hope and pray that I will do the best I can to help other people because anyone can satisfy their own desires. During the past week the greatest fear I've had is not forgetting what I truly want to do in life: be successful, work WITH people and work on becoming a better listener. Anyone can talk. However, you don't learn by speaking. You learn by listening," Bob declares in a slow but confident manner to those present. When finished, his parents smile with great pride. They know their son well enough to know he is sincere.

"Once again thank you all for coming today. I really appreciate everyone's help and support, particularly the generosity of the state of Illinois," Bob concludes his remarks to the applause of his family, friends, and media present. He is smiling from ear to ear.

"Oh, one last thing which I nearly forgot. Tracy and I have to return to school to complete the second semester. Since Tracy and I are strong supporters of education, we want to urge all of Illinois' school children to stay in school.

"Sometimes it is hard to complete our school assignments. Spending time with our friends or engaging in doing other non-productive activities can indeed be very tempting. . . Kids, if you're viewing this listen for a brief second. Despite the fact I am a millionaire, I have chosen to stay in school and complete my Masters Degree requirements. Someone once told me that you never stop learning. The thrill of the quick buck will never escape us all. Just keep your heads high and believe in yourself. You may not be the best, but do the best you can. In the end, God willing, everything will work out," Bob states.

As they were leaving, Jim grabs Bob by the arm and pulls him aside. "You really handled yourself well today. I spoke with a few reporters after you finished your speech. They were very impressed by your composure and how you answered their questions. It's not easy being in the public limelight. You conveyed a very positive impression about yourself," Jim states.

Bob smiles at his friend and replies, "Thanks for your kind remarks. Things did go well today. I really appreciate all your help in preparing the documents and getting everyone here. I will call you by the end of the week.

Upon returning to school for his spring semester, Bob was greeted by EVERYONE. Many of the students at school live in the Chicago area, so they had learned that he won. People who came across Robert Hamlin, whether a friend or not (there were people who disliked him for each of us know people with whom we disagree), recognized his face from the newspaper photos and TV interviews. Bob had become an instant celebrity. The key for him was not to permit his recent success to go to his head. Nor should winning the lottery be used as an excuse not to complete his course work.

His roommate Kevin was particularly happy for Bob. He was not able to attend the event staged with the media due to the death of a relative. Bob called him that same evening. He just wanted to make sure Kevin was okay emotionally. "Buddy, your call just provides another example of what type of person you are. Many people say they care; you go out and show it," Kevin declares.

Periodically over the holiday break they discussed the subject of winning, but Bob preferred to keep the discussion and relationship as things were before his recent luck. However, after returning to school, they addressed the topic in a more serious matter.

"Bob, knowing you as I do, I am sure you do not want to discuss this. So if I ask something that is uncomfortable, just let me know. Everyone is bringing up the topic of you winning. What I wanted to ask is, despite your financial problems being over, how are YOU doing? I know you're wealthy, but how are you?" Kevin inquires about his close friend and roommate.

"The past three weeks have really been something. I can now buy anything, yet I haven't worked for the money. Everyone knows who I am, but I haven't done anything. Hell, even when I won, the computer did all the work by me playing the quick Pick option. My involvement has centered on dealing with the luck of success, not the pride one would develop from knowing my wealth came from working hard with long hours to establish a business."

"Don't get me wrong. The feeling of being admired, respected and wanted is really incredible. The offers I have received from people the past three weeks are something else (Kevin smiles from what Bob is hinting at), and NO, I won't discuss them now. Deep down, I feel people are greeting me the millionaire, not me the person. People come up to me and say things like Boy, it must be great to be in your shoes. And they're right, it is. Sales people for every conceivable company call to sell this and that product. But it also is a great responsibility. But I also feel good about being in the position to help people with their problems," Bob states.

"You know, I never even considered that. In the papers and on television, you look so happy," Kevin affirms with a smile.

"Well, I am happy. But don't let anyone tell you it doesn't change you because it does. . . I haven't been the same since I won the game. Sleeping at night does pose some problems. Just when I think I can relax for a moment, the phone rings. It became so bad the first week that I asked my Mom to tell people that I was not home. It does not make me happy to blow people off," Bob states.

"I understand. You're the last person to be rude or not take the time for other people. It must be hard on you," Kevin replies.

"It is. I just wanted a break from the celebration, not to run away. People are only being curious, but after a few days it wears on you. I'm happy as hell, however, to be here at school. Just six weeks ago I did not want to return. I was really feeling the stress from exams, term papers, endless deadlines, etc. . . Now I'm ecstatic to be here." Bob states in a calm voice. Kevin notices that Bob's eyes do show a lack of sleep recently. They look bloodshot despite the fact that he no longer drinks alcohol. "Having to smile all the time. . . I feel like Ken doll, you know, Barbie's friend," Bob whispers as both he and Kevin laugh.

After they regain their composure from laughing, Bob continues the discussion. "Seriously, I've got something else on my mind. Even though the last three weeks have been stressful, they've also been the happiest of my life. I now look forward to school and homework that will soon begin again. My schedule should be much easier, with fewer term papers and assignments. Don't expect me to become Socrates or gain inner peace with myself now, but I really think things will be easier for me... AND everyone who has to deal with me," Bob declares. "I won't have to deal with Regan (his former professor) again . . .Big relief" Bob says while rolling his eyes.

Kevin smiles at Bob's last statement. "That's so cool! Last semester I was really beginning to worry about you. But in fairness to you, you DID mention that things would be fine once the semester ended. I am very happy for you. If my family or I didn't win, better a person like you. At least you'll do something positive with the money. And don't worry buddy, I have no intention to ask you for any money," Kevin proclaims as he and Bob start to laugh again.

"I know. That's why I took the liberty to get this," Bob states. He pulls from his desk drawer a cashier's check payable to Kevin for $1,000 and hands it to him. "You're a good person. Go buy yourself something nice. . .Pay off a credit card or get some new clothes," Bob says. The entire time Kevin just sat there completely shocked by his friend's generosity.

"When I run for the U.S. Congress in a few years, I want you to run my campaign. And believe me buddy; you'll be in for quite a ride. You'll probably become the best paid political consultant in the nation," Bob proclaims with a smile.

"Run your CAMPAIGN? Who are you kidding Robert Hamlin. I know NOTHING about politics," Kevin shouts as he slaps Bob upside his head. Even with all your money, you would lose with me running the show."

"Well, maybe. You're really good at working with people. Your composure and writing skills are excellent. Hell, you are a communications major right? You may feel that you don't know much about politics. However, you DO know quite a bit about public speaking, writing, being calm and motivating people. If that does not spell POLITICS (Bob glides his finger across Kevin's head, as if he is spelling the word), then I'll have a hard time learning what does," Bob tells his closest friend.

"Enough talk about that garbage. It's getting late and I'm going to bed. . . Just wanted to say it's good to see you again. I know things may seem tough, but they could be far worse. Sometime soon the questions will end and you'll be able to get on with your life. By the way, your recent luck could not have happened to a nicer guy," Kevin asserts while slapping Bob's shoulder.

"Yea, but I still am the second best person who lives in this room. . . with or without the money!" Bob repeats, always wanting to have the last sentence. Even when paying someone a compliment, Bob wanted the chance to have the final say.

However, Bob's wish was denied when Kevin spoke up and said "that's right Bob. You are the SECOND BEST person here and don't you ever forget it." Both of them laughed, probably because they both respected the other.

The second semester of graduate school began much like the first. His schedule consisted of four classes, each having its own set of requirements and assignments. One class studied how state and local governments finance their operations. Although political from the standpoint of learning what happens when certain taxes are raised, it had a strong flavor of both macro and microeconomics. To most college students, the word "econ" struck fear in their hearts. It was a nightmare most college students had been through at least once. Bob had taken both classes earlier in college. Nevertheless, it had always been a struggle for him.

Of all the classes while in graduate school, Bob found his Judicial Process class to be the most rewarding. The course focused on the decision-making process and history of the U.S. Supreme Court. Each student was asked to give three presentations based on particular readings they were assigned. "Court decisions and legal interpretation are important. However, what really moves people is the power of the spoken word," Bob whispered to himself after completing his speech requirements.

"The mouth that motivates people to act is the mouth that runs the economic and political structure of our nation. . .You're good at getting up before people and talking," a classmate told Bob after observing that his public speaking ability had improved dramatically. He placed his arm around Bob's shoulder to add emphasis to his statement.

After countless hours of reading books and writing reports, Bob took his knowledge from completing his graduate course work. He now was ready to take his comprehensive exams to earn his Master's Degree.

Chapter Twelve
Life's Exams Are Comprehensive

To complete his Masters Degree requirements, Bob had to take and pass three cumulative tests. He scheduled these three exams to be on Monday, Wednesday, and Friday of the week. Part of preparing for these tests included researching previous exams that other graduate students had taken within the last two years. Doing so provided strong insight as to what questions to study.

"Why is finding a place to study so difficult?" Bob whispered to himself. About two weeks before his tests, he had an encounter with two students from a local high school at the public library. Bob tried to be patient in the hope that they would stop talking or leave. After ten minutes, he could not take it anymore.

"Pardon me. . . I have been here for the last two hours. I am trying to study for some upcoming tests. Could you please be a little more quiet or go somewhere else to talk?" Bob asked with a calm but direct tone in his voice. It would be safe to say that he was polite, but there was NO misunderstanding that he wanted them to be quiet.

"Well, we're sooorrrry," one of the two females replied. "We will be more quiet just for you," she replied with a real smart tone in her voice.

"After all, this is where we ALWAYS talk!!" the other remarked. They tried to resume talking, but Bob got up and joined them at the table where they were talking.

"Perhaps the two of you misunderstood me. Let me explain this in another manner. This is a public library, not the ladies' bathroom. If you need to discuss who likes who, who thinks who is cute or who slept with who on 90210, that's fine. But please, do it somewhere else. . . I am not joking. Before you came here, you told your parents you would be studying when you BEGGED for their permission to come here!" Bob declares.

Both young ladies shrug their shoulders and start to laugh. However, they do not have too long to get comfortable. Much to their surprise Bob gathers some of their books and throws them into the open window, out into the rain outside. Bob sits back down and leans toward the girl who spoke first.

"But. . ." she replies.

"No time for tears. If you listen hard enough, you can hear your Mom calling you. At this time you have a golden opportunity to make a mature decision and go somewhere else to continue this discussion with your friend," Bob states.

The two girls gather their REMAINING items and leave the building. As one girl collects her wet books outside the window of the, she cries out in a whimper, "You did not have to be so mean. If you had politely asked, we would have been glad to go."

Bob then closes the window and states "Glad to have resolved that situation. As we just learned, sometimes kindly asking TWICE does not work. Sadly, difficult situations call for drastic solutions. I do not think they will be bothering anybody in the near future in public libraries," Bob states shaking his head.

The weekend before his exams, he was a nervous wreck. After dinner on Sunday, he took his fourth warm shower of the day in an attempt to relax. As he turned off the lights to go to sleep he mumbled, "God willing, combined with a good night's rest, things will be okay tomorrow."

The following morning, Bob departs the apartment shortly before 8:00 a.m. He could drive, but decides to walk instead. "This may be the longest walk of my life . . . Maybe I can get rid of some of this nervous energy," Bob states.

After passing Perkins Hall where he will be taking his tests he goes over the bridge and arrives at the library. Twenty minutes later, he realizes that he cannot concentrate. Bob proceeds then to the bathroom, partly to relieve himself, partly to calm himself down. "Why are you so upset?" Bob shouts while asking himself. "You have a test in two hours that you have been studying for three months now. You have been here for two days. Stop joking around and take the damn test!!" Bob exclaims.

Bob picks up some food and crosses the long bridge separating him from a graduate degree. At the department office he is handed the exam and some "blue books." These are white paper notebooks stapled together. They are used for taking college exams with long essay questions. Their covers are frequently blue. Upon review of the six questions for the test, Bob is ecstatic. The three areas he studied extensively have been selected as three of the six questions. "Passing means answering three of the six questions correctly. Passing. . .that's the goal today," Bob states in a rather upbeat and assertive tone.

At 4:20 p.m. he turns in his completed test with ten minutes to spare. During his return walk home, he notices how beautiful the weather is. "It's 60 degrees, the birds are chirping, and the angels are singing because I just kicked ass on test number one," Bob declares while walking down the street enjoying the spring-like scenery. At the apartment, a frozen pizza for dinner and another warm shower await him. However, by no means is he done for the day. He now has to begin studying for his second exam to be held on Wednesday.

After successfully finishing his exams later in the week, he went to the local flower shop and purchased three roses, one for his girlfriend and her two roommates. He wanted to show his appreciation for allowing him to stay free of charge in their apartment. Bob wrote a brief note to each which read: "Words alone cannot describe my gratitude this past week. I really appreciate you allowing me to stay here to study for my tests. If you EVER need a favor from me, do not hesitate to ask. Love, Bob"

Two weeks later he was notified by mail that he had passed each of his three exams. He soon began to consider his future. It reminded him of a discussion he had six years before with his mother. "You need to decide soon what it is you want to do the rest of your life. The clock is ticking, as in passing YOU by," Mrs. Hamlin shouted. As with most Mothers, he soon discovered that she was right.

However, what had changed was the luck Bob had recently encountered by winning the lottery. He was now in the position to start making decisions for the long term. He and Tracy had been dating for four years now and it had been more than a year since his lottery fortune began coming. After some thought, he came to a tentative conclusion as to what he would do . . . Tentative because he still consulted with Tracy regarding most actions he took. "Maybe I'm practicing for the future," Bob whispers.

Bob goes to the phone and dials her number. "Hey Trace, how are you doing?" Bob asks.

"I'm fine. How are you?" she responds.

"Got some great news. I learned today that I had passed my (Masters Degree) tests," Bob says in an upbeat manner.

"Yeaaaaa!" Tracy replies as she always does when hearing good news. "Way to go hon. I'm very happy for you!"

"By the way, what are we doing tonight?" Bob inquires. ""If you do not have any plans, there is something I would like to do."

"Oh yea!" she states as they both laugh. "Well, we don't have any plans. What do you want to do?" Tracy asks, her curiosity level increasing by the moment.

"Been doing a lot of thinking today," Bob states.

"Yea. We have talked about how thinking is dangerous to your health buddy!!!" Tracy shouts. She continues to tease Bob during the next few moments. Bob has grown used to her and others' teasing. Bob, of course, is very educated, but sometimes acts as if he lacks common sense.

"As I was saying. . . I thought some more today which would be a little more than yesterday, of course. In doing so, I have made some decisions," Bob states (while Tracy continues to laugh in the background). "How would you feel about going out to dinner tonight? Perhaps go to the 'Italian Town' Bob asks. The restaurant was their favorite. They both liked Italian food and it was not very expensive. Despite having a lot of money, Bob was still hesitant to spend any of it.

"Bob that would be great. We haven't gone out to dinner recently. We also seem to have problems spending time together," Tracy says. Bob had completed graduate school, but Tracy was still at school for her last semester. "While I was on spring break at home, you were at my apartment studying," Tracy states. On this particular weekend, she returned home to spend some time with Bob. She aspired to kidnap him and lead him toward the mall.

"Going out to dinner tonight will be good for the both of us. After all, we BOTH have a lot to talk about," Bob affirms in a confident voice.

"What do you mean by a LOT to discuss?" Tracy inquires. She'd been wondering for the past two months when their relationship was going to move beyond dating and into the Engaged Era. "Have you bought me something? Tell me, tell me, tell me," she says. Tracy had been entering the 'ready to settle down' phase over the past six months.

"Well, how would you feel about me going to law school or starting a business?" Bob states. She feels that he has REALLY dropped the ball until he says "I also want to talk about us. . . our relationship," Bob states in a somewhat nervous voice.

"All right, way to go Bob. You and I, together. How did you come to that conclusion? Was it published in some journal somewhere that only you would read, like Politics Today?" Tracy asks while laughing. For Bob, missing even the obvious was not beyond him. "Anyway, I would LOVE to go to dinner. Will we be going to our usual spot?" Tracy asks. Once Bob found something he liked, he rarely changed from the routine. He kind of followed the cliché "Why fix it if it wasn't broke?"

"We both like Italian food and we have a place we like. . . However, tonight I am willing to try another place. Somewhere else as long as one condition is met. . . We can go anywhere, as long as we do NOT go to that same restaurant you chose before," Bob declares.

"Heeeyyy, what do you mean?" Tracy inquires, speaking as if she is caught completely off guard. "I like eating there."

"You KNOW what I mean. The food is horrible. It's overpriced and there is no privacy," Bob replies as Tracy cuts him off.

"I LIKE it there. Besides, what does money have to do with it, Mr. Lottery?" she asks.

"Money has everything to do with it. Some people have incorrectly assumed that having money allows you to be a jerk, buy friends, or think you are better just because you can afford the country club membership. Pretending to be wealthy can be complicated. At least when you are born rich you have a right to be an ass!" Bob declares. Sorry about swearing, but the food IS bad. The lasagna was horrible. You know, you were there. If money is not an issue, like you stated, then I'd like some privacy while eating. I don't like wondering if the people next to us can hear our conversation. For some privacy and GOOD FOOD, I do not mind paying for it. The 'Cafe Italiano' you like is NOT an option tonight" Bob whispers, almost like he was concluding a speech. His feelings lead Tracy to feel disappointed. After all, she LIKES eating there, even if Bob does not.

"Okay," Tracy repeats again. "But what if I choose another spot to go to?" she innocently asks.

That's fine, as long as you pick a spot where we can talk. I just don't want to be the guest of audience participation time," Bob replies in answering her question. "Anywhere in particular?"

"Yes, but I am not going to tell you. It will be a surprise, unlike your attempt to keep a secret and surprise me. In that game you fail EVERY time. Your success level at trying to give me a surprise is '0 for the relationship,' Mr. Statistics," Tracy declares while laughing. "I'm sorry hon, but I just thought I would answer your question using the same numbers format that you've used to dazzle me and everyone else your entire life."

Well I can't surprise you because you don't allow it to happen. You always say 'Oh tell me, tell me, tell me.' You're always so GAME to be surprised," Bob replies with a very content laugh in his voice while rolling his eyes.

"Anyway buddy. I will pick a NICE place to eat in an attempt to please you. Do not ask where we are going. Try to look surprised. How does being here at 7:00 sound?" Tracy asks.

"That would be fine Superhon," (one of Tracy's nicknames Bob has given to her), "and unless some emergency happens, I'll be on time," Bob says. He is always on time, unless he is meeting with her. " We can go out and have a wonderful time together. See you soon," Bob replies.

"Keep thinking that. You'll get it right, someday," she states.

"By the way, I like dessert after dinner," Bob replies. Smiling, she knows exactly what he is talking about.

"Mom, I am going out with Tracy tonight. We are celebrating the successful passage of my exams. Also, we'll be discussing our joint futures tonight. It should prove to be very interesting," Bob states with a smile on his face. "Who knows what will happen."

"Did you purchase an engagement ring? I THOUGHT you had promised us Bob you would let us know beforehand? Do you believe he has done this?" Mrs. Hamlin angrily asks her husband. "Why were we not consulted?"

"What are you talking about? I have not bought a ring yet. Do you really believe I would go out and buy an engagement ring when both our families do not want the marriage to happen? Think for a second. Do you believe I, being wealthy, am stupid enough to give away one half of my winnings, (about $3 million over a twenty year time period) you're both missing the point!" Bob states while laughing. "You didn't raise any dummies."

"Well, that's good," Mrs. Hamlin curtly replies.

"As I have stated before, I will propose when I am ready and when I have decided who I will spend the rest of my life with. . . My marriage will not be prearranged nor am I requiring your stamp of approval beforehand," Bob states with a sigh. He briefly pauses before continuing and says, "I was really hoping that this issue was beyond this by now. Guess that is not the case. We're just going out to dinner. I am sure the topic will include our future together," Bob affirms.

"Well son, what do you want to do for a career the rest of your life?" Mr. Hamlin asks.

"Perhaps go to law school. I thought I would give it my best try to determine whether that is what I want to do or not. If after the first year I decide that is not what I want to do, I can move on. Have the luxury to try different things. The limited investments made in the IRA's and municipal bonds are doing well. I have paid off my debts and purchased a new car. Either that or I can open a nudist camp. I hear that has a lot of potential in the future," Bob responds with a smile. His parents' mouths drop down from the statement. "Believe me. . . I have come across too much money to have it wasted in paying a divorce settlement," Bob says.

"Nudist camp! Bob, are you serious? Never mind, you're changing the topic. What about the two of you? Where are things going?" Mrs. Hamlin asks, her face still showing a look of surprise.

"Tracy and I have been dating for nearly three years. It is time to consider whether we will be together in the future. It's only fair to her as to what we should do. I will say one thing, however. . . Tracy is a wonderful person, woman, and friend. Those qualities have been there for three years. I anticipate they will be there in the future. Wealth has not spoiled her. . . Believe me, not marrying her would only be one person's mistake: mine."

"She is a wonderful person and holds a special place in my heart. When I was in graduate school, I was not the most pleasant person. Through it all--- my homework, studying, preparing, etc.,--- she was there for me. Despite all the deadlines, meetings and school requirements, she remained very patient. I can safely say that whom I marry, it will be MY choice. It will not be requested, demanded, or asked of. . . I can only hope that in the future we will not have a similar discussion," Bob declares.

After a brief pause, Mr. Hamlin asks "Where are you two going to dinner?"

Mrs. Hamlin turns and offers her husband a strange stare. After all, she felt that the idea of who her son would be marrying was serious and not to be taken lightly. Bob pretends he is unaware of the tension by stating, "After some friendly disagreements, we concluded that she could choose the location, as long as it is not one particular Italian restaurant."

"Oh. . . What is wrong with that place? Are you being picky again? I thought you liked Italian food."

"The food is horrible and it is overpriced. There is NO privacy in the place. Everyone sits at tables where you feel like a sardine. For the sake of being kind, I will NOT identify the location. Regardless of these evident problems, Tracy LIKES the place. After going there once I decided that we would not return as a couple," Bob states with a laugh. "The place sucks."

"Watch your language, son!!!. . .Well anyway, I hope you two have a nice time tonight. As usual, you will probably have a lot to discuss. Tracy is a very nice girl. Do not get us wrong. We really DO like her. We just wish she were of the same religion," Mrs. Hamlin states.

"I know Mom. Thanks for your interest. You have both told me before about how you want me to marry a Catholic girl. However, the decision on who to marry should be mine alone. You can be sure that Tracy has heard the same concerns from her parents, so your opinions are not alone. Well, it is getting late. If you'll excuse me, I must be going . . . Even though I may not agree with you on this issue; I do appreciate your honesty. See you both tomorrow," Bob states as he gives both his parents a hug and kiss.

"Bob is a great son, but sometimes I wish he was not so damn stubborn," Mrs. Hamlin mumbles to herself in a low-pitched voice.

"What did you say hon? Did I miss something?" Mr. Hamlin asks.

"No, nothing," she replies. "He's just like his father."

Later that evening, Bob and Tracy arrive at the restaurant. After a short wait in the lounge, they are seated at a corner table. Tracy selected the location because Bob preferred to have his conversation limited to her and not the adjacent tables. Except for the occasional interruption by the waiter performing his job and for a baby crying a few tables away, their attention was focused on each other.

Bob grabs Tracy's hand and states, "I'm glad you wanted to go out tonight. I hoped to keep our discussion to US without the worry of the phone ringing or others talk."

"Well I'm glad you asked me. I love getting dressed up and going out to eat. Besides I really DO like being with you, I always have," Tracy answers him. The entire time they have eyes only for each other.

After placing their food orders, Bob resumes the discussion by saying, "I did some thinking today."

"You really have to stop doing that," Tracy says cutting Bob off. "The Surgeon General has determined that thinking is dangerous to YOUR health!" Tracy declares. Her statement drew a smile from Bob. Obviously her teasing did not bother him tonight. If Bob had not been feeling well or if her statements had disturbed him, he most likely would let her know.

"I was thinking about the future. I have tentatively decided that I would like to go to law school for one year. If that does not work out for whatever reason, then I will move on to something else. After all, I clearly remember what one year of graduate school did for my morale and attitude," Bob states.

"Oh yea! I remember that too. You were SO pleasant," Tracy states as they both laugh.

"As you stated, I was not the best company during that time. I can only pretend what three years of that treatment referred to as law school would do to my well being," Bob continues.

"You know me Bob. I have always supported you and will continue to do so WHATEVER occurs. But I have some questions. Why would you want to put yourself through that? You are a millionaire. You have all the money you need. Why put yourself through the agony of law school? Is it fame? Power?" Tracy asks. Her questions show a strong sense of concern.

"Just feel very fortunate. With all the money I won there are few financial worries. I now have the ability to do many things. However, I wonder if I was chosen. You know, if there is a reason why I won. Becoming wealthy occurred by luck, yet it allows me the chance to help others. It allows me to be charitable, but also aid the issues I care most about. Life would be a lot easier by being a couch potato, or satisfying only me," Bob declares in a tone even serious for Bob.

"I see. Well, what in particular would you like to do? What interests you the most?" Tracy asks of him.

"That I am not sure about. Perhaps running for (political) office would allow me the chance to help others. Being an elected official places you in the position, with large government budgets, to allocate money to help people deal with their particular problems. Listen to me. I was the one who hated politics. Now, I believe it's the only way one determines who gets helped and when," Bob states.

"Is money that big of a problem Bob? As you know, I am not too familiar or comfortable with politics," Tracy replies.

"Nor am I. But money is the root and cause of all evil in the world. People who have it, want more. Oftentimes they feel they must cheat or lie to fulfill their needs and in the end they are never satisfied."

"Politics is just an extension of all the problems facing society. It does pose one benefit, however. It allows people, if they choose to do so, to help other people and their needs. Well, enough about me. You said there were things you wanted to ask. What did you want to know? I really doubt it concerned politics," Bob states as they both laugh.

"You're right Bob. Another excellent perception of the obvious on your part," Tracy says while laughing. "You really know how to read a girl. We really have avoided this... but I want to discuss whether you think there is a long-term future between us. My family, especially my parents, asks me a lot about our relationship. They want to know the status of us and whether we are considering getting married," Tracy states as Bob interrupts her's laughing. A look of confusion is visible on her face.

"Come on," Bob states while trying to regain his composure. "Do not get upset. After all. . . you are ALWAYS laughing at me. This may surprise you, but I hear the same thing all the time from my family. The idea of you not being the same religion is one-half of what I have heard the past year from my family regarding you."

"What is the other half of the discussion?" Tracy sadly asks.

"How nice you are, despite that fact you are not Catholic," Bob replies as they both smile. "Besides, I always tell them I intend to marry who I want to. My marriage is not the culmination of someone else's plan of how we can arrange my life," Bob declares.

"And how do I fit in among your plans?" Tracy inquires as she holds Bob's hand.

"To be honest, it had not been a subject of thought until a few months ago. We both have been very busy with school and other things that occupy our time. But a few months ago I started to think that it would soon be the time for me to consider marriage. After all, neither of us is getting younger," Bob answers.

"And have you made any decisions about who that person may be?" Tracy then asks as a smile forms on her face.

"I think you and I should consider the idea of getting married. . . I haven't bought a ring yet, but I do love you very much. You are the closest friend I have. Our friendship was strong long before I won the lottery. Despite the many disagreements we've had, I miss the time we do not spend together. I hope you agree with me when I say I think we may have a great future together," Bob speaks clearly as Tracy begins to cry. "How do you feel about that?" Bob asks.

"I really think it is something we could both consider," Tracy replies with a large smile on her face. "Bob, I love you very much. As time goes by, I appreciate and respect you more. You are ALWAYS there when I need someone to talk to and you are there when I need help. I love you and I always will."

"Even, when I do something stupid?" Bob asks.

"That depends. What do you mean by stupid?" she replies.

Bob begins to laugh very hard at the question, which does not make Tracy very happy. "I'll let you figure that out with each passing day. Hey, I have an idea," Bob states.

"That's two now today, right? Please dazzle us with your discovery," Tracy states. She breaks out in laughter as Bob sits there with a strange, rather puzzled look on his face.

"How would you feel if we went someplace else after dinner?" Bob says. At times Bob may not be all too clear on what he means, but in this case Tracy knows exactly what Bob is talking about---and balks.

"Nope," she soon answers, not wasting ANY time. "Let's just continue to enjoy the pleasure of each other's company. I love being with you. . . I really do," she affirms.

"And if I want to get into politics. . . will you still love me then?" Bob inquires with a smile on his face.

"Don't push it!" she answers with a laugh as she grabs his hand.

Chapter Thirteen
Starting a Career

After some thought, Bob did decide to go to law school. He finished his final exams for the spring semester at John Adams Law School located in downtown Chicago. Academically he finished in the top third of his class, doing well enough to return for the second year. However, after receiving his grades he began to doubt if a career in the legal profession was his calling.

"I really do not think this is my future. Luckily I have the money to complete two more years of this, so it will not be a financial burden on me. However, the personal toll it is taking is starting to add up. Sleeping has become difficult. Tracy thinks I am a big bore because everything I do is law-school related. She is probably correct. And the stress from having to be perfect to be better than the competition is incredible."

"It is not that I am not up for the fight. Hell, I have ALWAYS been willing to work hard for what I believe in. I just do not think it is what I want to do. I don't feel comfortable doing this. There'll always be plenty of attorneys, but there is a shortage of good and qualified people running for elected office."

"Politics is what I'm good at. I really enjoy meeting people and being in the position to help others. More importantly, I also believe in doing the right thing. Standing up for what is right and fighting for the issues that help people, not enrich ourselves. Yea, that's me. That is exactly the boat I belong in," Bob declares. A smile soon develops on his face after reaching a conclusion about his future.

"There is an option about what could be done for a career. I am 24 years old now and I know what it is. It is time to get started on it. I will let Tracy know what I have decided," Bob states. Later that evening, he travels to her home. After talking briefly with her parents, he and Tracy go drive to Naperville, a large town a few miles west. There is a lake there where they enjoying walking.

"Hello hon. How are you?" Tracy says as they avoid some geese. "By the way, it is nice to know you still call me hon after all these years together. "

"I have made a decision," Bob affirms. It is a term he rarely used when making a point. Each time he uses it, Tracy normally laughs. His voice has a certain aura of confidence.

"Wow, another decision. That now makes three now this month, am I correct?" Tracy asks while laughing. "Bob, you really are a legend, in your own mind that is!!!"

"No comments from the gallery please. Thank you, we appreciate your support. Bob says to his girlfriend. "But on a more serious note, I think I have an idea as to what I should do with school" Bob says in a polite tone.

"What have you decided? After all, you and being serious. . . we would not want that any other way now," Tracy responds. She quickly removes the smile from her face when Bob remains quiet for a few seconds.

"After some thought I have chosen not to return to law school," Bob declares. She stops walking and the two are there, frozen, on the sidewalk. "I really don't feel I am cut out for the legal profession. It has nothing to do with not being able to do the work or if I could be successful. I do well in my assignments, writing legal briefs and speaking in public," Bob offers.

"What made you come to this decision Bob? Do you understand the consequences of what you are saying?" Tracy questions.

"Just do not think I would be happy doing it. Since money is not a problem, I want to do something where I'm happy," Bob says.

"If things are hard for everyone else, why do you feel you are exempt from the same problems?" she asks.

"Good question. We have the money to pick our careers. Balancing the family budget docs not depend on you or me going to law school. I am not suggesting we play couch potatoes and get fat. However, we can take the time to choose or prepare for a career that meets all of our needs, particularly our satisfaction and happiness with the job. Does that make sense?" Bob inquires.

"Sure it does. . . But you have not told me what you WANT to do," Tracy asserts.

"Soon after I won the lottery, I jokingly told myself that I would become a political campaign manager. I love the chance to meet new people. Networking and being involved in key electoral races is something I really thrive on. I know you don't share my feelings on this," Bob mumbles.

"Politics has NEVER interested me and my feelings have not changed," Tracy declares.

"But it is something I like doing. . .just like teaching is where your heart is," Bob replies. I have always supported you in your decision to teach. I hope you understand my opinion on this. I have decided to begin a political consultant firm. . .I have even come up with a title: The Campaign Focus Group. It will specialize in position paper writing, polling services, and campaign volunteer development," Bob states in a clear voice. The level of confidence and security in his decision are both clearly evident.

"You know how I feel about this. But, as always, I'll support your decision. However, I do have one request: You had better be the best or I'll get REALLY mad!" Tracy states. While doing so, she shakes her fist in Bob's face. She is not angry, she just wants Bob to know that she feared things would end up this way, even if she has no wish to be involved in the game of politics.

"I will never deny your career goals. You are great with kids. I know you want to be a Mom, but being a Mother will not be the culmination in your career."

"When I met you in college, you were studying to be a teacher. I have seen you work with children and you are FANTASTIC."

Tracy replies by whispering thank you.

"I have no intention to stop you from being the best, what third grade?"

"Yes," Tracy replies.

"Best third grade teacher there is. I know how talented you are with children. I only ask that you support me in my goals and aspirations," Bob patiently states to his girlfriend.

"Do you think you will ever run for public office?" Tracy asks, almost fearing the worst. After all, she has NO interest in the profession.

"I don't know," Bob replies. "Being the candidate was never the final objective for me in politics. Helping people was." After pausing to take a deep breath, Bob continues to talk.

"When I was younger, I really admired people who worked in the government. After watching the conventions," (he was referring to the Democratic and Republican National Conventions. They are held every four years the summer before the presidential election), "I told my Dad that is what I want to do. My father replied by asking what I was talking about. I told him, "I would like to be the person they are cheering for, the one on the stage."

"I came to realize that things were not going to be easy. After all, I was very shy in high school. Wasn't popular. Then developed a pimple problem in my college years. Since then I have learned that it costs a lot of money to run for office. For example, just running a credible race for the state legislature," (meaning having a chance to win) "in Illinois it costs at least $150,000. If you want to think about winning, you'll need more like $200,000.

"You almost have to be rich to afford to run. All of your time is spent raising money or campaigning at different events," Bob asserts.

"But you're forgetting something: You ARE wealthy. You have the money to do that," Tracy states.

"I know. That is what makes the decision to be involved in politics much easier. Paying our bills, earning a salary, buying a home and raising children," (upon hearing this Tracy smiles and grabs Bob's hand because she wants to have children) "can be done because money is not an issue."

"Our financial security does not depend on me being successful in politics. Do not get me wrong, I really feel I could do very well in the business. At least money will not be an issue," Bob states.

"Are there any other reasons why a career in politics interests you?" Tracy asks. She is not pleased with Bob's decision, but the tone in her voice indicates that her doubts have decreased.

"In these days, government is not looked on favorably. For a number of reasons politicians are not very popular. However, people also get what they ask for. All too often the ones who are the most truthful about what they want to do, such as Walter Mondale and Adlai Stevenson, (candidates who have lost elections for being accused of being too honest) get spanked on Election Day"

"I want to be a person who motivates people to get involved. Someone who people can look to and say 'I'm voting FOR him, not against him.' I may not agree with him on the issues, but I'll support him, because he's honest and he's someone I can trust. Does this make sense?" Bob asks.

"Yes it does," Tracy replies. "I think you would do well in politics. After all, you are a very good public speaker and you're very honest. But, you may need to work on keeping that temper of yours in control, buddy," Tracy says as she taps her finger on Bob's shoulder. "You have a lot of strengths. You're very good at doing research, investigating things and you can put down your ideas onto paper. I may not always show it, but I do know how you feel about politics. I hope this does not upset you, but I just am not as enthusiastic about it as you are," Tracy states. "Is that okay?"

"No, that's alright. I know how you feel about it. No one is saying you have to lead cheers about my career choice. All I ask is that you respect what I try to do."

"Look for a second at your choice of teaching. Today they are asked to be a counselor, friend, day care worker, and teacher all at the same time. If you asked them to turn around, you'd probably find a red cape like Superman's hanging from their neck.

They are asked to do all sorts of things PLUS teach the students. A degree in psychology would be needed, in addition to instructing the class.

Rest assured, one reason I have delayed proposing is because I wanted to be sure you were the right person. I do not want us to become another statistic. But as time goes by, regardless of what people want me to do, I love you more. As the months pass, I start to feel the day of our marriage drawing closer," Bob states as he grabs Tracy's hand.

"That is one of the sweetest things I've ever heard you say," Tracy says while smiling as she fights back the tears. "That really means a lot to me."

"You mean a lot to me," Bob answers as their hands draw tighter together. "I am taking my time so we can finish school, allow us both to be sure we are doing the right thing. Doing so will allow us to grow closer together. Since the topic is now out in the open, perhaps we should talk about our futures. . . what would happen, if we were to get married," Bob states.

"We have some obvious differences in our religions, children, work goals, etc. What I just mentioned are not minor differences of viewpoints. What do you think can be done to narrow the gap?" Tracy asks. The sound of her voice reveals how seriously she is taking the issue.

"You're right. . . We really do have some things to work out," Bob responds as they both smile. "We both know this won't be easy. Let's continue to walk and enjoy the pleasure of each other's company. Maybe we can make some sense of this," Bob says.

"I'd like to try," she whispers to him as they begin to kiss.

"Campaign Focus Group," Miss Sharon Perry answers the phone. "Yes, Mr. Hamlin is here. Let me transfer your call, thank you."

"Hello, this is Bob Hamlin. How can I help you?" Bob announces to the caller. Bob did take the plunge into the political consulting business. Within four months of that night's dinner with Tracy when they discussed the prospects of their future together, business was booming. The phone rang frequently and most of the calls were of a serious business nature.

Three months later, however, pretending to be busy was no longer necessary. The requests for the services Bob's firm offered soon were becoming too numerous; in essence, he was swamped. When one client was asked why he chose to use Bob's service and talents over a competitor, he replied "Although Bob is very young for a political consultant (he was 24), he does have eight years of practical experience in the field of politics. He has volunteered to help (previously for free) in several previous campaigns. I picked him because he knows the business." Doing so allowed him to gather IOU's for the future and gave him the chance to network and reach out to other people of similar interests.

After some thought, Bob concluded he would need to hire one or two assistants. Business for Bob's firm grew quickly.

"Sharon, we may need to place an ad in the paper. We have a serious problem," Bob stated.

"What? I thought business was going very well. God knows I have been swamped from preparing these reports. Getting them done is near impossible. . . the phone rings off the hook," Sharon responds. She was a 22-year-old female who had worked as a receptionist for a temporary agency the previous two years. At 5-foot 6-inches with brown hair, to say she was attractive was an understatement.

"You're right Sharon, we have been busy. Business is going great. However, with all the orders for help we will have to hire some more employees. We may not hire anyone from the ads we place, but we still have to comply with the various laws that apply. I do have some names and phone numbers of people I went to graduate school with. Excellent candidates. They are really good," Bob states, the tone in his voice indicating he is thinking.

"Do you want me to call them? I can make the time to do so," Sharon inquires. In the back of her mind she fears more work.

"No, I will. Doing so will make it easier to ask for their help. But, what needs to be done is calling the newspapers to ask what their advertising rates are. However, WE are going to lunch first to celebrate the fruit of our efforts. Did you have any plans?"

Sharon indicates no by nodding her head.

"Okay then, let's go," Bob states in a firm voice.

Both Bob and Sharon enjoy each other's company. However, neither pursued any physical interest with the other because what grew between them was a strong friendship. Besides, Bob is looking for an engagement ring for his girlfriend Tracy and Sharon has been dating someone for three years.

"What if I had plans for lunch today?" Sharon asks.

"Then you would go with your previous plans. The worst thing to do is blow someone off for OTHER meetings. After all, they are making the time for you. There will ALWAYS be another chance to do what you really prefer," Bob replies. Their relationship worked well for both: neither felt sexually intimidated or personally annoyed by the other.

Unlike most people in their careers, Bob loved what he was doing. His job gave him the opportunity to help others, socialize, and enjoy himself. "Life does not get much better than this," Bob shouts as he taps a bottle of his non-alcoholic beer with a friend, the scene resembling some major company's commercial frequently seen on television. Within a year of operation, he had four new employees and things were going well. His personal life had remained the same. After dating for three years, he decided to take "the big step."

Chapter Fourteen
Wedding Day

"With this ring, I thee wed," Bob stated as he completed the remainder of his vows. It was May 27th. Bob and Tracy were finally getting married and was the happiest day in both their lives. After a six-month engagement, the long awaited day had arrived. Everyone's wedding day is one event they happily remember.

For Bob and Tracy the same was true. She cried from the happiness when he proposed, but was not surprised whatsoever. "I knew this was going to happen," Tracy said while fighting back tears when he proposed. "You can never keep a surprise from me. . . you ALWAYS give it away!" she declared.

"Well, perhaps if you did not constantly say 'TELL ME! TELL ME! TELL ME! TELL ME!' Not doing that would allow me a better chance to surprise you," Bob had replied to her. This day represented the same emotions of hope, anxiety, and happiness shared by any young couple.

"By the power vested in me by the state and as a servant of God, I now pronounce you husband and wife. You may now kiss the bride," the minister states to Bob and Tracy. They both move forward to embrace and kiss each other. The level of applause grows as they are introduced as Mr. and Mrs. Robert and Tracy Hamlin. They then walk down the aisle, arm in arm, followed by the wedding party to exit the church.

After the service, Bob's mother was glowing with happiness. Because Bob and Tracy have different religious beliefs, both of their families could not have the opportunity to host the wedding. "I really wanted to have my son's marriage blessed by our priest," Mrs. Hamlin stated. She thought about the words used by the minister during the service. "Years ago interfaith marriages were discouraged. . . even safe to say, looked down upon. It was feared that it increased the chances for failure. Parents feared what faith the children would be raised into."

"Bob always spoke of how his religion would not interfere with the commitment needed in a successful marriage. By respecting my wishes to have the marriage blessed (by the Catholic Church) he has really made me proud! Tracy is really a wonderful person. . . I hope things are successful for them," his mother affirms with a smile.

At the wedding reception that evening, the best man was successful at making everyone laugh. Kevin, Bob's former roommate in college, wasn't trying to be a comedian in giving the wedding toast. He described some events that they had shared over the previous five years. Guests present laughed the entire fifteen minutes Kevin spoke. "He comes across as someone very stiff: no mistakes, strictly business, too serious. A true natural. To other people, he often comes across as a goof. As a neutral observation, he would cause most people to laugh and shake their heads. If he were running for political office, his Secret Service code name would be Simple," Kevin declares as the crowd laughed. When Kevin announced he was ending the toast, the crowd responded by booing. Quite simply, they loved his speech. All of the stories described were true and Bob was always easy to poke fun with a strong sense of humor. At its conclusion, Bob got up and hugged Kevin, laughing with the rest of the crowd.

Bob and Tracy had announced in their wedding invitations that they did not want any gifts. After all, they already had enough money from when he had previously won the lottery. However, since weddings are a time of giving, they did indicate on a separate letter that any money donated would be given away to charity. "We're having a drawing at the reception. Whatever charity's name is chosen will receive all of the donations from our guests' gifts," Bob privately announced to his parents and a few members of the wedding party.

Nearly $5,600 was collected from those willing to participate. As their guests arrived, they were asked to fill out a piece of paper listing their favorite charity. Later that evening, after the newlywed couple's first dance together, the flower girl joined them. Megan, a distant cousin of the bride, drew the lucky charity's name from the hat. "And the winner is, the Thomas Fund," the DJ shouted out to the crowd.

"For those of you who may not know, Baby Thomas is a young child from Chicago who needed a new heart transplant immediately after birth. To offset the expected cost of $300,000 for Baby Thomas' family, Bob and Tracy will give a check for the entire amount of tonight's cash gifts. They want to thank you for your help and generosity," the DJ declared.

The dinner was spectacular. The food was fantastic and the view within the hotel was beautiful. Slightly after midnight, the newlywed couple said their final goodbyes to their guests. They went upstairs to a nightclub located in the hotel above their reception room to enjoy three last dances together. They thanked the members of their wedding party for their help, then departed for the evening. "Hey Bob, if you need any ideas as to what to do tonight, feel free to give me a call," one of Bob's friends from college yelled. The rest of the people who remained began to laugh.

"No, I think we'll be okay. Go get some sleep. You won't have to wait for a call tonight. . . it ain't coming'"" Bob replied with a smile.

The following day they departed for their honeymoon. They had planned to be gone for two weeks. The first two days, they went to Galena, Illinois, a small town located a few miles east of the Mississippi River in the western part of the state. They also planned to make brief stops in Rockford and Freeport, Illinois. Complete with quaint little shops on Main Street that encompass all types of gift items, Galena is a town full of history dating to the Civil War. "I love going there," Bob replied when asked why he was going there on their honeymoon. "The people are wonderful. Plus, it's a great place to relax and play golf...to recharge our batteries" Bob says before going to the final stop: Hawaii.

After arriving in paradise they called each of their parents. "We just wanted to say hello and thank you for all your help. We truly appreciate your participation and help in on our wedding day," Bob and Tracy expressed to both their parents. After ten days of swimming, sightseeing, and spending a lot of private time alone, the happy couple returned home to O'Hare Airport in Chicago. The time together was very fulfilling but both were exhausted. They took one more day off to relax and thus begin the rest of their lives together. Bob returned to his political consultant firm and Tracy returned to the serenity of her third grade classroom located in Orland Park a South Suburb of Chicago.

"It's good to have you back here. Did you have a nice time on your honeymoon?" Sharon Perry, Bob's secretary, asks with a smile.

"Yes, we had a great time. We both really enjoyed ourselves. If you ever get the chance to go to Hawaii, take advantage of it. Perhaps the day will come when your boyfriend will propose. Who knows, if business continues to go well, you'll get a bigger wedding gift from me," Bob says with a smile. "I can't say I missed you on my honeymoon, but I always enjoy the opportunity to see you. Thanks for welcoming me back. What's on the schedule today?"

"You have a few appointments, but there is one here that puzzles me. Most of your clients and friends tell me what will be on the agenda when I make the schedule. However, one person did not. His name was James Wilson. Who is he?" Sharon asks with a puzzled look on her face.

"He is an alderman from Tinley Park, a town in the South Suburbs. Most people know him as a successful attorney who gives a lot of money in political campaigns. At my wedding reception he mentioned to me that he wanted to talk. However, like you learned, he did not want to bring up the topic for discussion. He only said that he would call during my honeymoon to set up an appointment. Hmmm, I wonder," Bob states. He looks more confused than Sharon was a few moments before. "Well anyway, what time is he coming?"

"At ten this morning. He asked for me to allow for at least an hour's time to talk with you. The whole arrangement sounded rather strange!" Sharon affirms in a clear voice.

"I guess we'll learn what he wants to talk about. Thanks for keeping things in order while I was gone. By the way, where are Pat and Thomas?" They were two of Bob's associates in the firm. Pat was a political campaign junkie, whom Bob had met three months before. Thomas was a fellow college graduate of Bob's school. Despite Thomas' more conservative political beliefs, Bob welcomed his presence in the firm because of his ability to win Republican political clients. "Bob likes to work with people, rather than against them," Thomas was once quoted as saying to some political opponents of Bob, as to why he was joining Bob's firm.

"They haven't come in yet," Sharon replies. There is a slight amount of hesitation in her voice.

"When they get here could you have them stop in. I want to hear how their various projects are going. The wedding is over and it is time to return to business," Bob replies with a wink of his eye.

"Okay, I'll tell them," she answers.

Shortly before ten in the morning Sharon knocks on Bob's door. Bob yells for her to come on in. He is on the phone trying to obtain a minor project for the business. The project would be small in size, but larger in the general scheme of the goals of the firm.

"Mr. James Wilson is here to see you Bob," Sharon states.

"Great! Tell him I will be right out to meet him. It will be about three minutes," Bob answers. Sharon took that to be about five minutes from her experience. Bob, however, took great pride in receiving clients and visitors at the office personally. He would ALWAYS leave his office to greet them in the lobby. The meeting would then be conducted in a separate conference room. After offering his guest the choice of where to sit, he would place himself at a chair to the side, never in the "intimidation chair" or behind a desk. He tried to treat everyone as an equal by having them feel more at ease, making it easier to work together.

Bob surprised Sharon by coming out early. Upon seeing Mr. Wilson, he immediately extended his arm and offered a firm handshake.

"Jim, it is really good to see you. Thanks for coming. We will be meeting in the conference room today," Bob declares in a firm voice. "Could you please bring some water, pop, and coffee. I'm sure Jim has a lot to say today. Thanks."

As they exit the lobby, Bob and Jim continue to extend their greetings to one another. They arrive at the conference room and settle in to talk. Bob leaves the door open because he knows Sharon will soon be returning.

"Well Jim, I doubt you came here to comment on my tan from the honeymoon. How can we help you today?" Bob asks.

"Thanks for making time to see me. I didn't' want to bring this up before your wife and friends. What I want to tell you is very important," Jim says as Sharon walks in with the refreshments.

"Let me help you with those," Bob states as he gets up to lend a hand. "Thanks. Could you please hold all my calls Sharon, but if my wife calls let it through," Bob whispers to her. He sits down to listen to what Jim has to say today.

"Bob, I've known you a long time. You worked hard in school, had a great deal of luck winning the lottery, and have what looks like a very successful business. You're a good person. . . We need more people like you," Mr. Wilson states.

"Thanks for your kind remarks. They mean a lot," Bob responds.

"I've spoken with many people the past two months. In doing so, I have heard nothing but kind and encouraging remarks about yourself, your wife, the business, your family, etc. You have a lot of good strong roots in place to keep your head on straight," Mr. Wilson says in complimenting him.

"Thanks again. But, I doubt you are here to nominate me for some award today. Is there anything I can help you with?" Bob asks, trying not to get swallowed up by Jim's flattery.

You may not want to hear this, but would you like to run for Congress next year?" Mr. Wilson says with a sincere look on his face. Bob's answer is not what he was hoping to hear.

"HA-HA-HA. . . HA-HA-HA-HA. . . HA-HA-HA-HA-HA-HA. . . Jim. . . I apologize for laughing, but I am going to respectfully decline. Don't get me wrong. I am not laughing at you or anyone else. But I've got to be honest with you. I simply have no intention to run for elected office right now, particularly to be a U.S. Congressman," Bob states to answer Mr. Wilson's question.

"Why is that?" Mr. Wilson asks. His tone indicates a strong level of surprise that Bob would have no interest to serve in the congress.

"How many reasons do you need? Ok, I just got married. My wife has no interest in politics. Believe me, NONE. Just discussing it brings a look of disdain to her face. Secondly, I began a business

111

about one year ago that is just starting to do well." Bob was being humble; it actually was quickly becoming very profitable.

"Quite frankly, I like things just the way they are. I really LOVE my job. I get excited about helping to elect people who share my concerns about what government can do to allow people to help themselves. To be truthful, the job's great and I would like to stick with it. Plus, I just returned from my honeymoon. Bob whispers.

"Are there any other reasons or doubts why you do not want to run?" Jim asks. The question really caught Bob by surprise. After all, most people let up when they hear two or three replies of no to the same question.

"I just don't care to run. I spend enough time away from my wife now as it is. I love her company. Actually, she's the better half of our relationship. Seriously though, this business requires at least sixty hours per week and I give it all the attention it deserves.

"Also my free time is very important to me. Running for elected office would eliminate the enjoyment I receive by spending quality time alone with my wife. Worst of all, I would be running against an incumbent. Congressman David Treadwell has been there for what seems like forever. Despite my differences with him, I would not stand a chance. He is well known and is much wealthier than me. Besides, he EARNED his money, I won mine'" Bob declares in response to Jim's inquiry.

"The points you made are well founded and I truly respect your honesty," Jim states as he places his hand on Bob's shoulder. "However, you may not be aware of one thing. Congressman Treadwell is not going to run for reelection. He has health problems that have not been made public yet. I heard the rumor three months ago and have been trying to verify the story. My sources have confirmed the rumor to be correct.

"Recently I have spoken with numerous members of the political community in the south suburbs. They include prominent attorneys, civic activists, elected township and school officials, and other key people. They are all open to the idea of your candidacy. With your consent to run, I can guarantee a primary election win in the spring. With the right type of money, volunteer support, and other tangible campaign donations, we can start in ten days," Mr. Wilson affirms in a clear voice.

"What do you mean by us? Jim, I really have no intention to run. I do not intend to spend my money to buy an election. Ross Perot may be bored being a billionaire, but I like what I am doing in my career. I much prefer being in the position to help others run who share the same views that I hold very dear to me. My wife does not want me to run for the school board, let alone the U.S. Congress. Having a good marriage is hard enough without the stress of a political campaign," Bob says. He is trying very hard not to let his emotions get the better of him.

"Alright, but could you think about what I said?" Neither you nor your wife may like the opportunity at hand, but you can win this election. At least try to confirm what I have stated about the congressman's health. . . that should be a starting point to see if what I have stated is true," Mr. Wilson replies.

"At this time in my life, I am not the right person for the job," Bob replies.

"Watch the news tomorrow night. An announcement is expected. You will be hearing from me (and others) again in the future. We want YOU to run," Jim affirms once again in a clear voice. "Do not be mistaken: this race is winnable. We will keep in touch."

"'Thanks for coming. I will bring up the subject with my wife, but do not expect a statement of my candidacy," Bob answers.

Bob gets up, shakes Jim's hand, and he escorts Jim to the door.

"Thanks again for sharing that information with me today, Mr. Wilson. . . We will be talking soon," Bob says.

After Jim had been gone a few minutes Sharon Perry speaks up. "What was that all about? Do you have a new client to support?"

"They have selected a possible candidate to run for Congress next year. You won't believe who the winner is," Bob says.

"Who is it? Is it someone you disagree with or don't want to win?" she asks.

"Worse. . . They want me to run," Bob replies with a look of fatigue on his face.

Later that evening, the bottom dropped out. "THEY WANT YOU TO DO WHAT?" Tracy Hamlin shouts. "Politics I thought was your job. Helping others to get elected. Remember? Wait!. . . Before this goes any further, what did you say?" Tracy asks. By no means is she happy from what Bob has stated.

"I told him we weren't interested. I stated no, but that I would run the idea by you, to see how you feel. . . I knew this would not take long. "We met today and I stated very clearly that I running was not an option at this point in my life. I told him we had just got married and that entering any race would create problems," Bob whispers as he places his arms around her. Bob did not mention that Congressman Treadwell was in poor health. It would not have made a difference anyway.

"Dinner is almost ready. Why don't we sit down for a moment and start the discussion over," she says while walking away. "Now, can you calmly explain why they want you to run?" Tracy earnestly asks. Her tone indicates that even her profound level of patience is being tested.

The next day during the evening's news does nothing to ease the tension. Bob arrived home and the story described how the Congressman had announced his retirement earlier that afternoon. Jim was off by one day. Surrounded by his family and friends, the ten-term incumbent declared his resignation due to poor health from a bad heart condition.

At that point the phone rang. After hesitating to answer it, Bob reached down to answer the phone. The voice he did not recognize, but the topic of conversation was very familiar.

"Do you have the television on?" the voice stated, Bob not yet knowing who he was speaking with replied, "Yes I do. I am watching the news. What subject should I be listening for? Who would this be that I am speaking with? The voice eludes me," Bob states.

"I understand you had a meeting with Jim Wilson yesterday. He is a close friend of mine. My name is Ted Krimmons and I am an attorney. I specialize in divorce cases, but I live in Chicago Heights," a suburb twenty miles south of Chicago. "Bob, do not be alarmed, I am sure you have many questions about why you are being approached to run for office," Mr. Krimmons states. "I apologize for calling you at home. However, I wanted to make clear that there are a key number of influential people across the South

Suburban area that supports your candidacy for the now vacant seat in Congress. We appreciate your time and willingness to consider all available options in this very difficult decision. As you know, they removed the age requirement to be elected president." It was done while Bob was a junior in college, about six years earlier. "Don't think for a moment that age should prevent you from running; you are as qualified to run as anyone else in this district," Mr. Krimmins states.

"PRESIDENT! This afternoon it was the Congress. That's quite a leap isn't it for a 25-year-old?" Bob asks. "I truly appreciate your generous offer. However, I have no intention to run," Bob responds as he motions to his wife that he will be off the phone shortly. "Running my business and beginning a marriage occupy enough of my time. Tell you what, you can be sure we will be discussing the subject the next few days. But I strongly advise that you look for an alternative candidate," Bob states.

"We will, Mr. Hamlin. After all, stranger things have happened. Remember, the Cubs (the professional baseball team) won the pennant last year," Mr. Krimmins speaks as both he and Bob laugh. The joke provided a brief break from the tension.

"Keep your options open. You may not fully believe the opportunity that awaits you. Being a U.S. Congressman is not something that happens to everyone. We are prepared to spend whatever money is needed for you to win. The seat is not just for anyone," Mr. Krimmins says as Bob finally cuts him off.

"Thanks for your time and help. I don't meant to be rude, but my wife and I have not eaten dinner yet. We both thank you for your concern, but my wife deserves my attention too, especially in our home. Good night Mr. Krimmins," Bob states as he politely hangs up the phone.

Bob turns around to face his wife and says, "Well they weren't joking. This is just the start. We have an unlisted phone number and they called. . . perhaps they think we will give up." He sighs after finishing the statement, his face becoming more depressed by the moment. "I'd love to run, but it's not the right time?" he offers, finally extending his wife the truth about his feelings.

"When I married you, I vowed to love you in sickness and in health. But, I did NOT promise to support a career in politics. You know I hate this. Damn politics. We just finished our honeymoon. Why us?" Tracy asks as she sits down. Two minutes later she begins to smile. Two years from now, I'll kick myself for this. I know deep down it is something you care very much about. We're not going to fight over this. I knew this would happen but was hoping it wouldn't happen for about... ten years. If you run, I will support you. But I cannot help you if YOU do not want it. If I help you, it has to be because it is something you want to do, not what everybody else wants," Tracy says with a sigh as she drinks some White Zinfandel. Her heart is not supportive of this idea at all.

"You'd really do it? I mean this will not be easy on us. It will require a great deal of my time; time I would rather spend with you. This race would put a great amount of stress on our relationship. We will be out shaking hands, giving speeches, kissing babies," Bob says as Tracy cuts him off.

"NO, the kissing of babies is my job!!! I am the one who loves kids, remember?" Tracy says with a smile on her face.

"Yea, but I'm the one who's running for office," Bob states.

"Oh yea. . . who says only you can run for political office? Last time I checked you didn't have a monopoly on the business. Who knows, maybe I would want to run to. Am I out of my mind? Tracy says. The two of them break out in laughter. Her hatred of politics would never allow her to ever consider such an idea. Hugs and kisses are exchanged between the two as they cuddle together for a long time. Although neither will admit it now, both know what Bob's decision will be about a possible campaign.

Chapter Fifteen
Diving Head First Into the Battle

"It is with deep respect, honor and pride that I introduce to you today OUR next Congressman of the 4th District of Illinois, Mr. Robert Thomas Hamlin," Mr. Wilson shouts to the roar of the crowd. The noise is deafening. Much to the surprise of Bob and Tracy Hamlin, a large crowd is gathered in the Oak Room of the Park Hotel in Homewood. The credit for producing such an audience would go to James Wilson.

After about two minutes of loud and sustained applause, Robert Hamlin tries to speak from the podium. It took some time for him and Tracy to walk through the throng of reporters, financial supporters, and friends gathered this evening. The entire crowd is clapping to a song titled "Is There Something I Should Know" the same song Bob and Tracy when entering the room at their wedding reception. No room could have contained this mob of people. Mr. Wilson and some key other people had delivered on one promise tonight: their ability to tap into Bob's level of support. Bob wanted a large crowd and he got one.

"Thank you. We greatly appreciate you'll coming. Our gathering today was originally scheduled for this morning, but I chose to delay it until this evening. This way, everyone who wanted to attend could be here. By the way, how we all doing tonight?" Bob asks. The crowd responds with shouts and applause, indicating their approval.

"I want to make clear that this is a campaign for you all, regardless of your social, economic, and political backgrounds. I am not running as some pawn being put up by anybody, particularly anyone who thinks a seat in Congress is for sale by the rich and powerful. If I felt otherwise, we would not be here today pledging each other our time and effort," Bob states. After completing his sentence, the crowd's applause forces him to pause before continuing with the speech.

"Before I address some concerns some of you may have and discuss the issues that have prompted me to enter this campaign, the same problems that affect this district and the state of Illinois, I have some people to thank. In politics, most people thank their wife and family last. I'm different from most people I know," Bob says, prompting most people in the room to laugh. "So, I want to first thank my newlywed wife. We hardly had a chance to unpack from our honeymoon when I was approached about running. So we must thank Tracy for allowing us to be here tonight," Bob says. She is intimidated by the crowd's size, so she moves closer toward Bob's side at the podium. The crowd chants in unison "Tracy, Tracy, Tracy."

"We could talk for the next twenty minutes of my appreciation, but I just want you all to know how much I value your support. Despite a thunderstorm and tornado warnings throughout the area today, I'm pleased to report that over 500 people are in attendance tonight," Bob states as the crowd erupts with applause.

"You know, since my age will be an issue in this race, I'll bring it up first. After all, my opponents will if I don't. Some people will contend that a person only 25 years of age should NOT be a U.S. Congressman. Young people lack both the number and level of life experiences, they may say. These, same people will say that young people should be disqualified from elected office. They believe we do not know how to manage money, cannot run a business, do not pay mortgages, etc. "

"Quite simply, the critics will argue that a 25-year-old cannot possibly offer solutions because they have not been here long enough to see the problems that confront us. If that is indeed your belief, then my speech is not for you and your time here today is wasted," Bob declares as the crowd chuckles in scattered laughter.

"I do pay a mortgage. I own a modest $130,000 home. As a down payment, I deposited $35,000, and the bank financed the remaining amount. Last year, nearly one year ago today, I began a political consulting firm known as the Campaign Focus Group. The firm was created with money I won from the lottery. The company is doing well and is profitable. These facts won't persuade the critics, but they do show I can manage money well.

"Also, I'll be upfront about how I acquired my money. Some people have advised me that it is no one's business how I came about it. However, I have decided to tell everyone. I felt you would prefer for a change someone running for public office (Bob would never allow himself to be called a politician) who wants to be honest with you. . .rather than lie or place the notorious 'spin' on the truth. Not too long ago, I was the co-winner in the Illinois State Lottery. My share of the winnings was $6 million. It is paid in equal yearly installments over a twenty-year time period. I am not poor.

"In being candid with you about my finances, I want to demonstrate something about me as a person. I could have taken the money and run. As a young and single person at the time, there were countless things that could have been done. I COULD have been out satisfying myself or doing nothing for the various charities I am lucky and grateful to be associated with. There is a trustee designated to make sure the appropriate amount of money is presented to those charities that I am lucky to be helping. They were chosen for their record of improving the lives of others while keeping to a minimum their administrative costs.

"These matters are important. There are countless Americans every day who give of their time and efforts to make this a better society. In our nation, however, many people have lost faith in our elected officials. Whether it is the waste of government spending or renewed stories of criminal behavior, some change is needed. The taxpayers, the working class, the self-employed, small business people---in essence, all of us---all deserve a fresh outlook from our elected officials," Bob states. Sustained applause breaks out from the crowd.

"Yes, trust will be an issue in this campaign. You deserve the right to know that your money is spent wisely. You deserve a government where every person, regardless of race or creed, has the opportunity to do the best they can, not just the rich and powerful," Bob declares while raising his fist high into the air. The audience breaks out in cheers. He was advised to take the high road and keep his emotions in check. After all he is young. People will expect him to convey how he feels with emotion, but with dignity. For a brief moment, he intended to let everyone know how serious he felt.

He then stops to regain his composure. "Before I describe what issues should be addressed, I must offer a voice of compassion. I have been a close follower of the political system for a long time in my short life. I offer, as I hope each of you does, my support and prayers for Representative Treadwell and his family. We all may have had differences in policy over the years. However, his record of service to the area, concern for the community and his endless energy will not easily be repeated by anyone. As we gather tonight, may we keep his family in mind as we move forward," Bob offers as the crowd heeds Bob's request to be courteous.

"This campaign begins the battle for the future of our nation. I want to work with everyone who wants to provide a certain level of support and dignity to protect our elderly in the golden years of life. In the same way, I will work to eliminate the benefits from those Americans who are millionaires receiving payments from the federal government. Wealthy and retired Americans have earned the benefits they presently receive. However, Social Security was established to provide financial security as we enter retirement, not as additional income for those people who do not need it. People have the right to live in dignity, God willing. However, those seniors who do not financially need the money, should not continue to receive something on the premise that 'somebody owes me.' Saying this is not popular, but leadership requires doing what is right, not what gathers additional votes," Bob states. The crowd remains silent. Obviously doing what is right is not always particularly the popular thing to say.

"I intend to work for an expanded trust fund for American college students. When I was away at school, I witnessed too many of my peers having financial difficulties. Most of these students came from lower to middle income families. The burden of working 40 to 60 hours per week, attending class, and doing homework often requires some tough decisions. Dropping out of school or cutting back on the number of hours worked, too frequently, is the only option a student has. After all, there are only 24 hours each day."

"Today's students are forced to borrow thousands of dollars per year to stay in school. Being hit with college debts of $20,000 to $30,000 is no way to begin a career. Businesses or potential employers have access to running credit checks. For too many families today, this debt is all too common of a problem. Also, it's no way to begin a marriage, placing additional stress on newlywed couples when the divorce rate is high enough as it is."

"Quite frankly, it is no way to prepare a workforce to compete with children from the rest of the world. The other industrialized nations of the world pay for THEIR children to attend college so they can be prepared for the jobs of the future. Their students don't have to decide between eating and making a student loan payment. Because of these loans our students frequently accept jobs that pay better at the expense of working with the poor, aiding our elderly or teaching our nation's school children. Since they are beating us in the world marketplace, perhaps they have something to offer us."

"What I will propose is the creation of a fund to pay for our lower to middle income students to go to college. The loan can be paid back in one of two ways. One would be a time-required period of service to our nation. There are many areas of need in America, all of which are worthy causes---that could use the help. The other means would be made as a payment as a percentage of a student's income. In this plan, the more the student earns, the larger the payment. It would, more importantly, encourage people to seek employment helping others, where perhaps the income is not as high, but the need for help grows daily.

"Despite some large costs, the fund could be self-sufficient. It's just takes vision in creating programs that work for everyone involved. Money raised would then be provided to each student who wished to participate," Bob states as the audience listens. "Now, I may be young, but I am smart enough to know such a plan will generate a lot of opposition. All too often, the best ideas that allow people to help themselves usually do. We'll all hear about the default rate involving student loans. I will also sponsor an amnesty program not currently available through banks. If for eight years you make the minimum payment on-time or pay off at least one-half the principal borrowed, whichever is larger, the remainder of your loan will be forgiven. If not, the student would continue to pay under the previous terms until the loan is satisfied."

"Doing this has two key features. One, it rewards the payment of the existing term of a loan. If you show responsibility by fulfilling your end of the deal, such an effort should be rewarded.

More importantly, it could help remove some credit problems that many young people face when buying a home, car, or other large appliances. Reducing the loan is not intended to avoid existing debts or avoid responsibilities. For those people here who are old enough to remember, the period in our history with the greatest period of economic growth was during the 1950's. The government paid to educate our veterans from the Second World War. Education is not an expense; it is an investment in our future," Bob says as the audience screams and applauds for thirty seconds.

"Personal responsibility should be addressed. Discussing it is not meant to win votes, but to encourage some common sense. When I was growing up I too became very good at pointing the finger, blaming everyone else but myself, making it known when someone else did wrong, etc. However, as I have grown older and wiser, I have learned that taking the blame is good on occasion. Doing so helps diffuse tension. We see the topic of blame in higher divorce rates and greater stress in society. Quite a few of our problems we could begin to solve by saying 'I'm sorry because I was wrong,' rather than filing more lawsuits."

"With each passing year the problems become greater. We need not look any farther than our children to see what has happened. We have kids who cannot obtain a driver's license, but are facing murder charges. Somewhere along the way, a lesser value of human life was begun. My parents had the same pressures (money, kids, a job, other people, mortgage payment, etc.) that confronted their peers. Luckily for my siblings and me, they made the commitment to us and to each other."

"At times I felt my parents had no clue as to what they were doing. I recall my mother telling me many times that when you grow up, I hope you have kids just like you," Bob says as the crowd begins to laugh. "I never knew then what she meant. . . but I do today. Every day I am reminded that most of my problems are caused by me: a short temper, impatience, and seeking acceptance from everyone."

"What we need to do is find a way toward reaching some common ground. All too often we blame THEM or someone else. Not being able to communicate with people of different races, creeds, generations, religions, and orientations only serves to pull us apart. I believe that part of being an elected official requires trying to improve the economic, educational, and political opportunities for everyone. But all of us, as a society, have to stop thinking of ourselves and work toward a better understanding of each other."

"For example, take the issue of crime. Eventually it hurts all of us; it is not just THEIR problem. Because society has placed a lower value on life, everyone has higher consumer prices, higher insurance premiums, and higher taxes to pay for a criminal justice system that is not working. Society has placed a much greater value on material goods. We're all paying more for these mistakes as the years go by."

"Many issues confront us as a nation. As well intentioned as our gun laws are, for example, they do not eliminate the shootings we hear about on a daily basis. The areas with the greatest rates and incidents of crime also have the strictest gun laws. The good people among us who wish to purchase a gun for protection or sport have the hardest time doing so. However, the thugs and criminals have always found a way to obtain weapons that protect their livelihoods and illegal activities. They would never register their firearm or try to obtain a gun permit."

"What we need is not just stronger laws, but better parenting. We need to show our children that life IS important, that life DOES matter, and that other people DO have something to contribute!!!" Bob shouts as the crowd roars its approval. Bob has to pause briefly as the audience regains its composure. Coming from a young person, his words really seemed to move people. Everyone in the crowd may not have agreed with his views, but they respected his opinion of people's need to accept responsibility for their actions.

"However that still is not enough. Parenting is important, but life is not that simple in itself. What needs to be done is make the use of a firearm during the commission of a crime, whether it is murder, robbery, or another felony, a serious offense. Society should punish those who misuse their 'Right to Bear Arms' against the rest of us. Give 'em ten years to think about the right they violated," Bob says as the crowd cheers their approval.

"I do support using the death penalty, and I have no qualms about making people's life uncomfortable in prison. However, you are more likely to be executed if you are a minority than if you are white and convicted of similar types of crimes. What I will support are sentencing guidelines for felonies: if you are convicted of X crime, then you will receive Y punishment. That way, regardless of whether you are rich or poor, black or white, tall or short, a more equal form of justice CAN develop. People may then start to place more trust in the criminal justice system. Cretins like O.J. Simpson won't walk free on murder charges because our documented examples of wrongful prosecution in the past," Bob states as the crowd roars with approval for about one minute.

"However, on no circumstance will I support showing such executions on television. Children are very impressionable, whether they are watching Barney, the Power Rangers or movies such as Lethal Weapon. Showing executions on TV will do nothing to decrease the frequency which crimes are committed. As a matter of fact, some evidence shows that the murder rate actually goes up during the week when the death penalty is implemented. It's hard to believe, but this stat shows that it is not just children who are impressionable. The same TV is being watched by thugs, rapists, and deviants who go out and commit other crimes after its glamorization."

"Something we don't hear much about concerns helping the law enforcement community itself. It is no secret that criminals and gang members are better armed than the police. Our officers, not the criminals, are the ones given the authority to protect us. They, not the thugs who control parts of inner city neighborhoods---and don't think they are not expanding outward into suburban communities---are the ones who need YOUR support. They need OUR help to testify against those committing crimes against society: the drug dealers, the murderers, the robbers, and rapists. Those who violate our desire to live peacefully."

"We, as a community, need you to serve on jury duty or testify when asked to do so by the government. Yes, what I am saying is that I am asking everyone here in the Fourth District to expand the basic definition of what we include as being a citizen. It's more complicated than standing before a large flag and saying 'I'm an

American.' I will lobby for federal legislation to force employers to pay your regular wage that you would have earned. You, who give of your time participating in the system, should not have to fear meeting your family budget earning $17 per day as a juror. The system as it presently works rewards people who try to escape their responsibility of being a citizen and it should be changed. It's why we have non-educated people determining the fate of criminals, or even worse, innocent people," Bob Hamlin says to an upbeat crowd.

"Let us now discuss some aspects of our economy. Part of what is happening requires some fundamental change. When we as Americans have to buy from other nations what we developed, it is obvious there is something wrong. For example, take the VCR. How many of you know it was first produced here in the United States? The company that created the VCR sold the patent to a firm in Japan. Maybe it was done to offset an expected loss that the business foresaw for the next quarter of that year."

"The company earned enough money to cover the loss, but they lost millions in potential profits because they were short-sighted in their long term corporate goals. Such activities are all too often designed to satisfy the stockholders. Selling the patent was an act that produced lost profits, closed down manufacturing plants, and decreased sales opportunities today, and broken families. In other words. . .stupidity."

"Worst of all is the impact on our young people. When a plant closes down, the hopes and dreams of children wanting to work in 'the mill' are gone forever. The impact of this is very strong. Not everyone is college material. When the plant shuts down, other noticeable things happen as well. The streets fall apart, city services such as police and fire protection decline, and the businesses surrounding the plant---whose economic stability is tied to it--- eventually fail as well."

"Bear with me everyone. I know this is a rather long speech, but there are many problems that face our district. These problems extend from Aurora to Chicago Heights and from Calumet City to Joliet. I would briefly like to discuss education. Critics of giving more money to the schools feel that we are just throwing more money at the problem. When too many students drop out as they do each year, the suspicion that our schools are failing is not wrong. Even those who do graduate lack the basic skills to read and complete a job application."

"Not only must we address the disparities in funding between the poor and wealthy school districts, but we must ask more of ourselves. I do not yet have any children so perhaps I am the last person to say this. However, I do remember when I was young. My parents made sure every night that I had done my homework AND that it was done right. Today, due to the change within the family structure, our kids are falling prey to the wishes of gangs and the television set. If we truly want to regain control of our economic destiny, if we want improve test scores, and if we want to better compete in the world market place. . . we must win the hearts and minds of our children. We must do SOMETHING that rewards parents who accept their responsibilities who teach children to do what is right, and who give their time to create a better community where they live," Bob shouts. The crowd erupts with cheers and sustained applause.

"I knew he was good, but wow… Incredible," State Representative Gilmore whispers to his wife. "You can't teach what he's doing. He has a grip on this crowd."

"Electing one person from our district will not solve these problems. Citizens have grown tired of false hopes and reams being tossed like Frisbees as answers. I only will make two promises in this campaign in addition to doing the best I can. Being an elected official, I believe, requires more than a commitment. The problems facing America do not run on a 9 to 5 shift. Many people work two jobs, but still most of their free time is on the weekend or during the week. If that is when THEY are free to meet with me or ask for help, a reasonable person would conclude that perhaps THEN is when some time should be made for other people's needs. Keeping such a schedule may place demands on my family life, but that is part of the responsibility of a public servant. I will meet with you one night a week, throughout the district. Let me be your sounding board," Bob says.

"My second promise concerns limiting my term as a Congressman. I feel that after six years in office if you do not have the same level of energy and desire to assist others with their needs, then you SHOULD step aside. I hereby promise to serve no more than three consecutive terms. That's six years. By that time I should be BURNT out, my family will be STRESSED out, and my fellow members of Congress will argue that I be THROWN out for trying to change too many things," Bob declares. The crowd politely laughs at his last statement and then begins to applaud very loudly.

"Once again I want to thank everyone for coming. The weather was horrible today, but I do appreciate your being here tonight. Luckily we didn't witness any severe weather today like some storms that have struck the cities of Oak Lawn, Plainfield, Roanoke or Utica, Illinois in the past. I truly am looking forward to seeing you in your neighborhoods, at picnics, where you work, at your children's schools, etc. You may grow tired of seeing me a lot. You may begin to think you're seeing a mirage: No, that cannot be Bob, I saw him earlier today. . . and two times last week." The crowd laughs as Bob finishes his statement with a smile. "However, if that does happen, it means that I am working harder than the opposition. We're gonna win," Bob says.

"Stand tall everyone. Keep your heads up. This will be a long journey in the year ahead. It won't always be fun, but it won't be boring. May God bless you all. May he keep watch over you and your families," Bob states as he bows and finishes his speech. The entire crowd now stands simultaneously and cheers in a loud sustained level of applause. Bob turns toward Tracy and gives her a big hug. He then greets individual members on the stage, providing each person with a firm handshake. About two minutes later he turns around to face the large crowd waving to as many people as he recognizes.

Within the hour, most of the audience had left and returned to their homes and families. One woman, a mother of four children in her mid-forties, turns toward her husband and asks, "Do you think he can win?"

Her husband, a plumber by profession, declares "I don't know. I have known Bob's family for a long time. He is very stubborn, but hardest working person I know. If he does not win this election, he will die trying," he responds.

"No. . .I mean, can anyone really change the government? Can anyone really make things better?" she asks.

"He may not succeed but it will not be because he didn't try," he says while escorting his wife to their car.

"Wonder how many other people are discussing his speech tonight on their way home," she states.

"Probably quite a few; Most likely, everyone. What a speech!!!... Did you notice how the crowd responded. I mean, he moved people. Hell, look at us," he responds.

"Have you ever heard a better speech" she asks.

"No. But there is something more important than being popular or a good speaker...He's honest. People believe him because he's a good person. For him, it's not just talk. It's a promise," the husband whispers.

Chapter Sixteen
Running For Political Office

"Good morning. How are you doing today? Have a great day. Good morning, I am Robert Hamlin and I am running for Congress. . . Nice to meet you," Bob states with a smile on his face. It is 6:10 in the morning and Bob is at the train station in Richton Park, Illinois. He is greeting commuters who work in Downtown Chicago, but live in the far South Suburbs. "Hi. Nice to meet you. I'm Robert Hamlin. I running to be your next Congressman," he states again to a new commuter. He is probably the 200th person he has already met this morning. What occurs when greeting voters is almost comical because we're meeting them at a neutral time.

It is now 6:17 a.m. Bob decides to step aside and let the remaining people who approach him to pass. After all, the next train arrives in three minutes. "The last thing I want is to be responsible for a commuter to miss his or her train, just to shake someone's hand. One person's vote is just not that important, regardless of how close the race will be," Bob states. He greets each commuter with a smile and a firm handshake. Throughout it all, his is fighting back "large" yawns, trying very hard not to let anyone know he is tired .

After all the excitement from the night before, he finally fell asleep at 2:00 a.m. Two hours later he awoke to go to the train station. Two young staff members, who had previously stated they would join Bob at the station, arrived shortly before six. One held a "HAMLIN FOR CONGRESS" sign, the other helped to give away literature with Bob's picture on it. Bob decided to schedule this event right away. There were other elected officials who would love to become the next Congressman. For Bob to win, which would be hard regardless of his age, it would require a minor miracle. First, he was unknown to most of the district's voters. Second, he had never run for public office before. "Putting together a staff, campaign volunteers, etc., requires a great deal of effort and money. How can we do it," Bob questioned when debating whether to jump into the race.

One of his volunteers named John began to yawn so Bob spoke up. "I'm tired too. We are in this race for the next year with the primary election in six months. This will not become any easier. Are your prepared to work and give up a lot of your free time and personal life? We'll be attending a lot of social events, but it won't be party time. You will receive the most rewarding education of your lifetime. We'll visit neighborhoods that you only see on the news. People really do live in poverty, which you'll see firsthand. I guarantee that you will NOT be bored," Bob declared with a strong degree of emphasis. "By the way guys, I used to do the same thing as you're doing now. Standing there with a sign, giving away brochures, greeting people...It's not glamorous, but someone has to do it. I know it is not fun getting up at 4 or 5 in the morning. Wanted to let you both know I appreciate your help. Thanks"

At 6:22 a.m., after the train had come and gone, Bob returned to introducing himself to the commuters. At this time, a van with the logo NCN printed on its side pulled up. NCN stood for "National Cable News." It was a surprise to his friends, but not to Bob. His staff had arranged for the interview after convincing the cable service that it was national news for a 25-year-old to run for Congress. Being 25 barely would have previously made him eligible to run for the U.S. Congress. The requirement was waived via an earlier amendment to in the U.S. Constitution a few years before. Now anyone, who is of legal age to vote, became eligible to run for any federal office. However, he was still younger than any of his "potential" opponents entering the race.

"Good morning guys, I'm Robert Hamlin," Bob shouted to one of the employees from the cable network.

They were busy unloading their equipment from the van when one individual responded "We'll be right with you Mr. Hamlin. We just need to get our stuff," said John Rogers, the crew's supervisor.

"Don't worry, take your time. The next train won't be here for another ten minutes. You arrived at a good moment. . . By the way, my name is Bob," he shouted as his two volunteers laughed. "MR. HAMLIN, give me a break. Those two are older than me," Bob said with a smile as John and Rick laughed. "By the way guys, if you need any help unloading your equipment, just ask," Bob stated.

"No thanks Mr. Hamlin. We're ok," they replied.

Bob continued to greet the commuters as they approached the train station. "Good morning sir, I am Bob Hamlin," Bob stated as John handed him a brochure. John's partner named Rick was holding a Hamlin for Congress sign about thirty feet in front of them. "Good morning everyone!! Come meet Bob Hamlin today. . . he's running to become your Congressman," Rick shouted as a large group of commuters were passing him and approaching Bob. By 6:23 a.m., the employees from NCN were filming the scene.

"What's all the excitement today? What's happening?" a young female asked. By her tone it was clear that she was caught up in the morning's festivities. There are usually no TV cameras at the station, certainly not at this time of the day. By her pleasant voice, it was obvious she was used to being up very early in the morning to ride the train and was in a very happy mood.

"Hi. My name is Bob Hamlin. I want to be your next Congressman," Bob stated as he extended his hand to greet the young lady.

"My name is Trish and it's nice to meet you. Why are you here today?" she asked.

"We are here to get an early start in this campaign. Most people running for office come to greet you here the week before the election. I am running for a seat in the U.S. Congress, but am here one year before the election to show how serious we are. . . It's not about winning. It about making the effort to learn what concerns people by listening. Cannot fix these problems if we don't know what you, the citizens.care most about," Bob asserts. " Yea, I'm here today but more importantly will return in the future. I intend to work each day, before and after the election," Bob responds.

"It is nice to see you here. I'm sorry but I don't know who you are. Can I have something to read to learn more about you? It would be a nice change from sleeping or reading the paper. After all, most of the news I read is bad," Trisha declares.

"Sure. Here's a brochure, which gives a brief description about me. It has my picture on it to help you remember the face. You will be hearing more about our campaign in the months ahead. Trish, it was nice to meet you today Have a nice day!" Bob states.

"Likewise Bob. Hope to see you again soon. Bye." Trisha says as she hurries toward the train. The camera crew recorded the entire interview. Bob heard the sound of the horn from the train so he steps aside to let another round of last minute commuters pass.

From the corner of his eye Bob can see someone running toward him. A man in his late 30's is panting. He passes the five members of Bob's entourage, hurdles the turnstile, and gallops up the stairs toward the platform.

"I really hope he makes (his train) after all that effort. His job schedule must be very important. . . Jumping over the railings and leaping into a moving train whose door is closing just simply is not worth it," Bob whispers to himself. After all, the next train arrives in rush hour just fifteen minutes later. John, his associate, says "You know the way he cleared the railing he looked like O.J. Simpson. Remember those commercials in the airport. What grace. Go O.J. Go!" he said so only those nearby could hear. The others present smiled or laughed, but Bob chose not to. He stood there quietly. Bob had his own opinion about the allegations made in the criminal indictment and what was explained in what some call the Trial of the Century.

Bob was then asked by the camera crew to turn around because they felt it would create a better "shot" for the camera. Bob happily agreed, as long as no one from his party would be blocking the tunnel. Doing so would limit access to the stairs to reach the train platform. Hamlin knew from previous visits to the stations (after all, he too was as a daily rider to Downtown Chicago) that the last thing you want to do is upset someone early in the morning. When doing so, most people will not forgive you and they will tell anyone who will listen how some "Bob Hamlin running for something had caused him or her to be late for work."

The remainder of the morning was uneventful, which was good. It was only the second public appearance of the campaign, but Bob was very pleased with how things went.

"Guys, I thought things went outstanding. We gave away a lot of brochures. That's hard when twenty people are passing you at the same time. And we did it all without upsetting anyone. Well. . . almost everyone. Some of our "friends" forget that there is that little document known as the U.S. Constitution that permits us to be here, particularly the one guy we saw today talking about the value of freedom and then saying we had no right to campaign here. And he thinks I'm the Communist. Some people just don't get simple terms like democratic elections. He wouldn't have voted for me anyway," Bob says while the other two laugh.

"You know, getting up early is hard, but I enjoyed being here. Bob, do you have any other plans today?" Rick asks with a serious look on his face.

"Unfortunately most of my time will be spent raising money. Despite the fact I won the lottery, people think I can buy my way into office. Spend most of my time on the phone raising money. Being only twenty-five makes it even harder. Many think I am rushing into this. . . that I should wait my turn. People kind of resent someone who has money but never worked for it. It's probably a legitimate concern. However, these same people probably would be opposing me if I was thirty-five as well. For us to win, we've got a lot of work to do," Bob states.

"Do you really think you can win?" John asks. "It's not that you are a bad person, in fact I like you a lot, but. . . I just do not know the odds of you winning in your first try."

"You are correct. It is nearly impossible to defeat an incumbent Congressman unless he or she is caught in a drug or sex scandal. This fact alone helps to explain the success for the movement of term limitations. This race is for an 'open seat.' At this time nobody knows who our opponent will be if we win the primary. A lot of people, with a lot of money will be very interested in who wins this race."

"I am in this contest to win. There are more profitable things that could be done. In this business, winning is everything. Finishing in second place is as good as being last. Both are losses. There are severe problems here in America, particularly in the South Suburbs of Chicago. Someone, whether it's me or not, needs to lead the call for a change. However, I am not an elected official, have no political debts or IOU's to anyone, and do have enough of my own money to defend myself if the opposition intends to criticize who we are and what we stand for," Bob says.

"Who better than us to lead the focus for change? There are so many issues facing this state and our district that have been ignored for so long. We can push to secure a better future for everyone by working to resolve these problems that confront us now. We, as young people, represent the next generation of leadership. If I felt the problems facing us were being addressed. . . or if I felt that I was going to lose, I would not have entered this race. The costs of our generation not having a voice in the future of this nation are jut too much for us not to try," Bob declares.

"How much do you think this (race) will cost? Do we have a budget?" Rick asks.

"Winning this race will cost between $300,000 to $500,000. That's right. Three hundred thousand to be competitive, close to $500,000 to win. The worst part is that I, like every other candidate for Congress, have to spend more than half my time raising money. We should be spending our time listening to the voters, hearing what they have to say. Perhaps more people would participate if they felt that our elected officials cared about their needs, not what the special interests or the powerful want.

"Just think for a moment. . . $500,000! How many charities in America not only need the money, but also are in better position to spend it on people's true needs? The money would be far better spent on research for children's health care or buying computers for children who live in poor school districts. There are so many better ways to spend money than on electing candidates for public office. These crooks that have the nerve to take bribes and use the system to make them rich endanger the entire political system.

"Quite frankly, the whole process of electing our public officials needs to be changed. You have these people. They become too comfortable. Only after being indicted for criminal acts while performing their job are they thrown out by the voters after being there for what seemed like. . .forever. Over time, their understanding of basic needs of most people slips farther away. This is one reason why I decided to run for office," Bob states with a clear voice.

"How much could you really do? After all you would be only one of what, 400 or so members of Congress. Do you believe things would be done better if you were there?" his friend John asks.

"Probably not. However, I have always done the best I could at whatever I have attempted. The only fear I have is that they would throw me out," Bob states as all three of them laugh at the thought. "Imagine that, being removed for trying these problems. Trying to IMPROVE the current system," Bob repeats as they continue to laugh. "Guys, thank you for your help. I am going to get on the train and go to work myself. After all I have to earn a living too," Bob declares with a smile. He himself then ran up the stairs to catch HIS train.

After putting down his stuff, he traveled from car to car visiting with his fellow commuters. He heard a lot of complaints about taxes being high, fears about their children's futures, questions about making health care affordable, etc. One woman named Lois felt Bob was being hesitant to answer her question. After raising the tone of her voice, Bob replied, "Lois, I am not going to promise you anything or tell you what you want to hear. I am not the incumbent and most people believe politicians are full of lies anyway. Please let me listen to your problem. No one learns by talking. We each learn by listening," Bob stated.

After a brief pause the passengers began to clap. Watching a politician listen rather than talk was indeed a pleasant surprise, particularly at 8:00 in the morning.

After greeting everyone in each car, Bob turned around and said, "Thank you all very much for your time today. I apologize if I have interrupted your commute. I will see you all again, hopefully very soon."

When Bob returned toward his seat he is stopped by a woman in her early 50"s. "Mr. Hamlin, I want you to know you are a fine young man and I hope you win. Besides, my daughter thinks you are very cute," she says as many of the riders begin to laugh.

"Thanks. That's nice to hear," Bob replies, as he begins to turn red from being embarrassed.

The train arrives downtown. The ride was fifty minutes in length. Bob likes to watch people and the expressions they convey on their faces. Most are tired and some are angry. Some are hung over from drinking. A few choose to play cards. Others just lie there sleeping. The "cheerleaders", those commuters who know everyone in their car from their ride each day, laugh or discuss what's new in their lives. On this Wednesday, morning they proceed to enjoy themselves and entertain each other.

"It is too bad more people are not like them. I guess with the problems facing today's families and the world at-large it is easy to see why few people smile. Hell, I'm as guilty as the rest of them," Bob completed his sentence as the train arrives at Randolph Street Station in Downtown Chicago. In his brief walk from the train to his office, he notices another homeless person. It is the forth one he has seen today. "We all think our problems are bad... and they are. But there is always someone who has is a little harder than the rest of us."

Bob enters his suite and notices his secretary Sharon Perry still has not arrived. Shortly before 9:00 she comes in and begins to apologize.

"I am SO sorry I'm late. You will not believe what happened. . . It will not happen again," Sharon states. Bob has become used to her tardiness, but his compassion takes Sharon off guard.

"We are open from 9:00 to 5:00 Sharon. You are EARLY, not late. Besides I was late myself today. I was at the train station at 6:00 and was shaking hands with commuters who work here downtown," Bob answers.

"You were where. . . When?" Sharon asks. "I thought you would be sleeping in today for sure. You had a very late night last night with your speech and all. My boyfriend and I discussed what occurred afterwards. . . Did I hear right that 400 to 500 people were there? We were amazed by the turnout. I had no idea you were such a good speaker either. What you said... made us think. We talked for at least an hour after it ended," Sharon says.

"Thanks. However, I do not intend to come between you and your boyfriend," Bob offers as they both laugh. "One thing to remember, win or lose, everyone here will have a job a year from now. You can BET on that. We do not have to rely on elections to pay the bills here. By the way, I get caught up frequently in my own projects and our business. How are you doing?" Bob inquires.

"Great. Got a lot going on. But tell me about your event? That's more interesting anyway," Sharon says with a great deal of enthusiasm.

"Really well. Was excited about how things went last night. Because I was in the 'LET'S GO' mode, we decided to meet at the train station. However, there will be days in the next year that I don't want to get up and campaign. I once read about a candidate for president who became so flustered about what town he was in, he had to pull out the phone book in his hotel room to tell him. Politics can be frustrating at times. On the other hand, it is also a lot of fun. I love meeting new people. Doing it well is really an art. It requires a lot of practice."

"However, my age and lack of experience will hurt me in this campaign. Somehow. . .we need to turn this around and use the energy I have to substitute for age. Being twenty-five is very young to be doing this. The members of the local media sources are very concerned with what we are doing. Today's project is to call again all those contacts from the news sources. We need to schedule dates and times next week for exclusive interviews. It's very important is to make everyone feel they have direct access to me, particularly those who do not have the big dollars and can promise votes. As in life, the people who are most successful are the people who make EVERYONE feel important."

"The greatest fear people will have about me running for office now will be my youth and inexperience. It's easy to be an outsider, claim you'll 'shake up the system.' Most people grow tired of these pretenders. Most people over forty do not trust people under thirty. They have worked hard in their careers, have mortgages to pay, are beginning to plan for retirement, and are interested in providing a secure future for themselves and their children. They have earned what they have. It's not fair to label them selfish or petty," Bob declares. "What I or any candidate for office needs to show is that government CAN be used as a means to improve their lives and protect their investments."

"Also if you can please type this 'thank you' letter for everyone who came the night before. Each letter should be personalized, but feel free to edit it to make it conversational----like how you and I are speaking," Bob requested. He felt it did not take much time or effort to say thanks or to let someone know you appreciated their time and enjoyed the pleasure of meeting them.

"Unlike most people, you REALLY do take great pride in communicating with others," Sharon offers. Then, only to herself she thought, "Boy, Bob does care about other people's needs and feelings. I am glad not just to work with him, but the chance to know him. I'm proud to call him my friend."

"By the way, you provided a lot of help in preparing our event last evening. . . Everything was perfect and the turnout was higher than we expected. I never got the chance to say thank you," Bob declares.

"You're welcome," Sharon replies with a smile on her face. Bob used the term OUR to let Sharon know his satisfaction to make her feel included and take ownership for its success. Spreading the credit around is something we can all work on. "It does not take much effort to let people know that what they do is important—and appreciated. More people should try," Bob often thought to himself.

At 10:30 a.m. Kevin Chapin, his roommate from college, walks in. He works for a major public relations firm in Chicago. He is still one to two years away from being named a partner. Nevertheless, he is considered an "up and comer" there. He is well respected among both the firm's partners and associates. Such a trait is indeed rare in these economic times.

"Hi, can I help you?" Sharon asks of the good-looking man standing before her.

"Yes, you must be Sharon. I've heard many nice things about you. My name.is Kevin Chapin," he replies.

"Oh, so you're Kevin. Bob talks about you all the time. He's on the phone right now. Let me tell him you are here," Sharon responds.

"On the phone, that's typical," Kevin declares as Bob interrupts him.

"KEV HEAD. How are you today buddy?" Bob says while extending his arm to shake hands. "I thought you would be here at 10:28. This guy is a lot like me. He is always on time. Just one of the many reasons he'll be named a partner next year," Bob says in an upbeat manner.

"Don't take him too seriously. He and I have SEVERAL different traits. He's a great guy, but he is a lot higher strung than I," Kevin replies. Bob begins to laugh very loudly.

"You're right again. Nothing seems to slip by you. However, I am STILL happy you could stop by. After all, we have work to do," Bob says with a smile.

"You're uptight at times, but you can always laugh at yourself. Doing so is a character trait not everyone can say that they have, particularly those individuals who like to poke fun of other people," Kevin declares.

" Thank you sir. Sharon, we'll be in my office for an hour. Please hold all my calls," Bob states. As they proceed down the hall, Sharon gives Kevin the attention of her eye and mind. She is taking more than just a casual interest in him.

After a few moments the tension increases between Bob and Kevin. The disagreement focuses on where to campaign.

"Kevin, I feel we can best win by spending time in each area of the district. Whether black or white, rich or poor, every voter has needs. EVERYONE requires help at some time in his or her lives. Even wealthy people feel they need tax breaks. I want everyone to know I can be counted on when, for whatever reason, they feel they must turn to the government for help. I don't intend to avoid going to certain neighborhoods for safety or political reasons."

"I asked you to run my campaign because this business requires putting people around you who you can trust. I know politics is NOT your favorite topic. You can take comfort in knowing most other people hate it too. You have your own career. You're damn good at what you do. That's why I asked you to run my campaign. Win or lose, this race is not going to damage our friendship. I entered this to fight for the issues that concern me most. Winning is only a part to pursue that process. There will be times, like now, where we don't agree. Hell, you may even be right, from time to time," Bob declares as they both begin to laugh.

"As you know I was the PR major. You gave an outstanding speech last night. As a matter of fact, you did better than I had hoped for. You have a great business. . . a lot of people are supporting you in this race. But I have got to tell you: Many people will view you as being too young to be mayor, let alone a U.S. Congressman. Not me, remember! People over 50 will be most suspicious of you. . . or anyone like you. They will question your ability to solve the problems you discussed in your speech. They will, also, question your motivation for running and your sincerity. However, I lived with you for three years. I know you, and I BELIEVE in you. Yet, most of the voters, I fear, may not want to learn more about you," Kevin states.

"Ok. Do you have any ideas as to how to appeal to them? Or at least, have them listen to what I have to say?" Bob asks, his face showing how serious he is on this and most other facets of his life.

"You'll just have to outwork everyone else. You will have to attend all their events, visit them in the nursing homes, and attend every birthday. Some of your ideas may be viewed (by senior citizens) as too drastic. They will try to portray you as insensitive and unknowledgeable. You'll need to show you are human: prone to making mistakes, that you can laugh at yourself, and that there is no S on your chest (S standing for Superman). Then is when they will notice you. Show them that you truly do care. . . that you are not some slick salesman asking for ten seconds of their time in the voting booth. There will always be skeptics, but over time we'll see positive results. After all, I know the real you," Kevin responds.

"Thanks. It's good to hear that," Bob says. He is very much moved by Kevin's polite remark.

Later that afternoon Bob was scheduled to have lunch with three labor leaders. Bob had a personal policy not to leave a discussion when things were not going well, so he decided to be late for the meeting out of respect for his friendship. However, luckily Kevin made the decision easier by announcing, "Hey, I don't mean to rush off, but I am due at the office. I'll call you later to continue our discussion," Kevin stated.

After exchanging goodbyes at the elevator, Bob departed. The look on his face resembled that of learning that his dog had just died.

Two hours later Bob returned. However, his mood had gone through a complete 180-degree turn. "HELLO SHARON. I'M BACK. BOY… DO I FEEL GREAT! Nothing like a good meal to cheer me up," Bob shouted.

"So things went okay at lunch?" Sharon asked with a degree of hesitation. She had seen Bob immediately before he left and he did not look too well.

"HELLLLL YESSSS!!" Bob exclaimed in response. The smile on his face enlarged with each syllable. "However, I have to call Kevin. We may have a way to address the issue of my age," Bob calmly stated, his emotions having returned to a normal balance.

"You never mentioned Kevin was so good looking. I know you have other things to talk to him about. Could you just tell him I said hi and enjoyed meeting him today. . . And then tell me how he responds?" Sharon asks with a shy look of innocence. Her tone showed that she truly was hoping she had caught Kevin's eye without having to ask him.

"I never told you about my appearance but you figured it out, right?" Bob jokingly asks. "Don't fear, Sharon. I will happily let him know you're glad you had a chance to meet. I know you are seeing someone else, but you deserve the very best. But remember, until Election Day his attention is mine. Besides, I'm not sure if he is straight," Bob says. He smiled at her and returned to his office, laughing out loud.

Sharon just stood there, her lip nearly causing permanent damage as it bounced off the ground. "Is he gay" Sharon questions herself in Bob's absence.

Bob picks up the phone and calls Kevin. "Hey, it's me again. Things going good at work? I just returned from lunch. Hey, I wanted to let you know you're right about our discussion earlier. In fact, think I got a way to resolve the problem. Get this Kevin, from now on we will. . ."

Chapter Seventeen
The Time to Pursue the Future Is Now

". . . just be ourselves. During this last week of the campaign, do the best you can. You only live once. After all, this is just politics. It's only a small part of our lives. Important? Yes, but it does not run our lives and it will not pay the bills. We have the issues on our side. Deep down, we have the energy to follow through on our convictions that we hold to be true. . . Keep your heads up. When I entered this race a year ago, no one said winning was going to be easy," Bob stated his emphasis to some supporters.

The following week Bob stood before another packed room. It was the night before the general election, Monday, November 4th. Twenty-four hours later the polls would close. All the effort of the past fourteen months will have come to an end. Two hundred volunteers gathered at his campaign office. They were part of the 600 plus regiment of people who had all signed up to work two to 10 hours the following day to help Bob's voters come to the polls. Likely supporters had been identified by making phone calls and by going "door to door" in neighborhoods throughout the district.

"We stand together once again. Tomorrow evening we will learn whether our journey over the past fourteen months has been successful. We have rung thousands of doorbells, made only you know how many calls. We were not the picked favorite to win the primary election last March, but we did. In a field of six candidates we won with more than 52 percent of the vote. We defeated some difficult competition. Two of our opponents are current members of the legislature here in the state of Illinois. In fact, both are here tonight. Thanks for your support these past few months' gentlemen," Bob says in acknowledging his prior opponents.

"I know firsthand how hard it is to give of your time and money to a political campaign, particularly your free time. Many of you here have children, work at least one, perhaps, two jobs. There are other events and responsibilities that demand your time and effort. And, believe me whatever your demands, they are MORE important than politics or this campaign. Before we continue, I just want everyone to let all of you know how much I appreciate your help. I myself have been a volunteer in the past. Going from house to house, avoiding dogs and slammed doors in your face. Walking in the rain and cold, feeling very much alone, wondering as you go if anyone cares. I understand. I've been reminded each day as a candidate how hard it is and all that you have done for me because I do it too."

"I could not look you straight in the eye and ask for your help—and just sit in a warm, dry room and hope the money, volunteers and votes fall into my lap. If I did, you would probably view me with the same level of distrust and anger that most voters have for elected officials today. Thanks to you all, "Bob says as the crowd cheers wildly.

"We have been told many times the past year how young and inexperienced I am. We've been asked how someone, who has had so few birthdays and life experiences, can possibly know what life is about. How can some young person claim to have insight about the problems that face our country. I believe the experts were referring to me," Bob states as the audience laughs, " The answer, my friends, is that I have seen and heard the plight and problems that you face. On the day I announced my candidacy I made one key promise: To meet with the citizens and taxpayers of this district on THEIR terms."

"I am pleased to announce that we have met the promise made to YOU, the people of this district. I have attended over 40 school board meetings. We have gone to more than 150 neighborhood and homeowner meetings. We have eaten chicken at more than 200 picnics and I have given more than 400 speeches. We have visited more than 6,000 homes over the past year. We all have tried to meet with people on THEIR terms, at their convenience. The issues I have addressed are the problems that confront the residents of the South and Southwest Suburbs of Chicago each and every day."

"Please let me provide a few examples as I ask for your patience. A few of us visited the town of Ford Heights, (a suburb located about 25 miles South of Chicago along the state's border with Indiana.) It was once described as 'the poorest city in America.' The

Reverend Johnson accompanied us from the First Baptist Church when canvassing the neighborhood.

"We went to one residence occupied by an elderly woman. Before she could speak with me, she had to undo and release three locks on the door. What concerned her the most? Take the issue crime in our communities. She had never been arrested, but she was a prisoner in her own home. . .She had only three locks on the door because that was all she could afford. Her fear of just being able to leave her house confronts her and millions of other Americans every day. Her plight is why I speak about providing harsher sentences for criminals and for a Victims' Bill of Rights."

"We have visited with children at more than 60 events at local schools this campaign. My audiences have varied from school board members to students on government and civics. What surprised me the most? No, it wasn't the gang graffiti or the cracked playgrounds. It was the differences in the level of computer equipment, the paint on the walls, the presence of carpeting and other features commonly seen in a school. The differences in what types of computer equipment in schools located less than one mile apart from each other was incredible."

"Here's what we saw. Some schools had no computers, more than 40 desks in the classroom, and ceilings that were falling apart. Other schools had pipes in the rooms where the room temperature was 100 degrees. In the winter, the same room was 40 degrees with no hope of improvement for the foreseeable future. The radiator would make really odd noises. The teacher's job was, therefore, made that much more difficult. She could only TRY to yell louder than the radiator and other classroom disturbances." Because of what I have seen firsthand, I've visited our state capital in Springfield, home of Abraham Lincoln, to lobby the legislature to change how we fund our public schools and provide the necessary monies our ALL of our children.

"How can we expect all of our students to learn or compete with the children in Japan and Germany when they cannot possibly compete with the children attending school less than one mile away? Life is not fair. However, how can reasonable people permit a system to continue where schools located so close in proximity do not have anywhere near the level of comparable resources. The schools I saw just did not fall apart or become danger zones. . . or monuments to neglect in one day. It was NOT the work of some punk with a spray can; it takes time for paint on a wall to chip and for a ceiling to collapse."

"That is why I've been so outspoken to have the federal government have a greater role in providing the necessary funding for ALL of our schools where control over spending the money is kept at the local level," Bob shouts. The crowd applauds, with many school employees cheering much louder. After all, they not only see these problems everyday, but Bob was one of the few candidates to come and inspect these problems firsthand.

"I've traveled from Joliet to Calumet City and from Aurora to Chicago Heights. I've seen the plight of our communities after the decline of the steel industry. When large manufacturing plants close, it's not just the 500 to 2,000 people who used to work there who suffer. The hopes and dreams of their children suffer. Most often, they are forced to move away from the area - to find a career someplace else. Also, the services provided by our local governments are hurt from fewer dollars coming in because the tax base is depleted. The local infrastructure of our bridges, roads, and streets collapses, thus placing a greater burden on the businesses that remain behind."

"The economic problem eventually extends toward the local shopkeepers surrounding the plant. With less traffic in the neighborhood, there are fewer people to buy the products offered. In essence, we all suffer. Fewer people working, more people collecting unemployment, and the entire family structure suffers from greater financial pressures. Charities are asked to provide more help to greater numbers of our people. . . That is why I have spoken of the need to provide tax breaks to those businesses that continue to operate within certain depressed areas, and for grants to retrain our workers."

"I have also addressed the fact that Illinois is not getting its fair share back from the federal government. Our state lacks large military bases and has fewer defense contractors in comparison to other states. Therefore, our state does not benefit as well financially during those periods of a military buildup seen during the 1980's. It actually affects the entire Midwest Region. Since we don't have many military bases or defense contractors, our state does not share the same rewards from higher levels of defense spending. I'm not talking about being weak on defense. I'm describing that Illinois does not economically benefit as we would if we focused tax dollars on other avenues."

"It is my firm belief that Illinois benefits from more money spent on our infrastructure needs. Illinois relies heavily on transportation: We have the world's busiest airport. We have a state at least 300 miles long with roads in great need of repair. Hell, anyone who has driven in our state KNOWS what I am talking about!" Bob shouts as the crowd applauds. Many in attendance tonight used roads that are in complete need of replacement, for there are many streets located within blocks of this campaign office located in Kankakee, Illinois. The same situation existed in his other campaign offices located in Chicago Heights and Joliet too.

"Illinois benefits from what we call shared-cost projects. We are a wealthy state. Programs whose costs are 'shared' between the state and federal government benefit US! We can afford to participate in such programs because from a per capita basis, but this may not be reflective of the towns in our Fourth District, our state has more tax dollars than our counterparts in the Southern States."

We live in such a diverse state. These problems I just discussed are not limited just to our congressional district. The issues of school finance, property tax relief, road construction, and economic development occur throughout the state from Schaumburg to Ottawa, from Rockford to Western Springs, from Cairo to Brookfield, from Freeport to Oak Lawn from East St. Louis to Lombard, from Hinsdale to Rock Island, from Galena to Gurnee, from Wheaton to Waukegan and from Springfield, our capital, to Summit..." Bob says as the audience laughs. You get the idea. "In our college towns from Normal to DeKalb, from Elmhurst to Naperville, from Carbondale to Bloomington, from Evanston to Champaign-Urbana from Peoria to Chicago and from Charleston to Macomb we see opportunities in research and the energy of our young people to create a better future in technology to farming to pharmaceuticals," Bob declares.

The crowd rises to its feet in energetic applause and loud cheers of support.

Before continuing, Bob pauses to gather his thoughts again. "To make a long story short, there are a lot of problems facing this district and our nation. I say OUR district because we all have an interest in the area around us. I have lived in this area my entire life and I intend to stay here, win or lose tomorrow," Bob states as his voice begins to fade again. He takes a sip of water and takes a deep breath.

"We believe in you Bob because you believe in US, the people who live here," one person shouts as the entire crowd cheers.

"Thanks. This has been a long campaign. There has been mud thrown from both sides during this race. Being the immature and inexperienced person, you know the 'new kid on the block' as my opponent has called me," Bob states as the audience has a good laugh. The race has had a particularly negative tone, but most neutral observers contend that it has been Bob's opponent, State Senator Michael Simmons, who has thrown most of the negative "grenades" during the past few months. The term "New Kid" refers to the nickname Senator Simmons gave to Bob about four months ago, as his polling data showed the race was indeed tightening.

"The mere idea that I lowered the level of this race is garbage. After all, I had the most to lose by doing so. The fact that my opponent has helped secure government contracts for his friends, who in turn donated to his campaign, IS important. Such selfishness helps explain why fewer people vote each year. They simply do NOT trust people like the distinguished senator," Bob shouts. He remembered from a class in college the best way to insult your opponent in politics is by praising him.

"Last of all, I want to thank all of you. Not only for listening to me speak tonight and throughout the past year, but. . . for everything. Being young and never run for office before, I really had no idea what to expect. Your kindness has been remarkable. You've let me in your homes for a cold drink on a hot day, gave me food as I traveled in your neighborhoods. . . Hell, everything you've done. . . just meant so much to my wife Tracy and I. On behalf of my family,

I wanted to say thank you," Bob whispers as he begins to choke up. The crowd applauds to give him a chance to regain his composure.

"There really is no more I can do to win. YOU are the ones who have the ability to make history tomorrow. There simply is no more time. . . I will end OUR campaign by making one last promise: If you work hard for me during the next 24 hours, my wife, who has been the most patient saint throughout this endeavor, and I will work hard for you for the next 24 months. Thank you for everything. May God bless you and keep watch over you all and your families," Bob says to finish his speech. As he steps toward his wife and gives her a hug, all 200 plus people rise and applaud. Many have tears in their eyes, glad to have had the chance to meet Bob, but fearful about their chances of victory.

After two to three minutes of sustained applause, during which Bob was hugging and greeting everyone he could, he returns toward the podium. He places his hand over his eye to wipe away the tear that was forming. He finally shows a big smile to his supporters, who are still loudly cheering. Three minutes later after the clapping had stopped, a voice from the back yells out "We love you Bob!" Being prone to becoming embarrassed easily, Bob's face begins to turn red. Nevertheless, he smiles at the crowd once again. With his arm firmly placed around his wife, he says, "We love you too." The crowd roars its approval. Stan Thomas, a local member of the state legislature who Bob had defeated in the primary, grabs the microphone and begins shouting "Hamlin, Hamlin, Hamlin, Hamlin!" as the crowd responds in kind.

After saying goodbye to everyone, Bob escorts his wife to her car. He has asked Kevin to stay behind so they could talk for a few minutes. Each had a beer in their hand: Kevin a draft beer and Bob an alcohol-free brew. After grabbing their beverage of personal choice, they sit down and begin to talk.

"Kevin, I just wanted to thank you for all your help. You never were in a campaign before, but you were fantastic. You did a great job. Regardless of all the fights we've had, our friendship has held firm. . . Thanks buddy," Bob states as Kevin smiles.

"Bob, I've put together some numbers. They are based on a minimum turnout for tomorrow's election of forty percent. Based on vote totals from previous elections, you'll probably lose by 800 to 1,200 votes. You have narrowed the gap a great deal; after all you were behind by twenty points in our own polls. You're running against a state senator who has represented nearly one half of this district for ten years and who declined to debate you. What you have done is simply amazing during the past two months. NINETY PERCENT of the undecided voters are breaking your way. . . If we had one more week to campaign, we'd win, hands down," Kevin sadly says. The tone of his voice got lower the longer he spoke.

After reviewing the figures for some time, Bob asks "Is there any chance for us to win?" His reply was both good and bad news on the topic.

"You are in a great position to run in two years. However, those people deciding now are breaking toward us in huge percentages. If all of them vote and this is a big if, the turnout is higher than fifty percent, we may have a chance. We've done some great things. We've registered more than 3,000 new voters, for example. The best advice I have is... pray for a sunny and warm day. If the turnout hits 53 percent, we'll probably win. But that rate is almost unheard of," Kevin softly replies.

"What's the possibility of doing that, getting a turnout around 55 percent?" Bob sadly inquires.

"Well, we've created a GOTV (Get out the Vote) organization where over 600 people tomorrow will be helping you. There are some pretty competitive races in the district, notably for the state senate seat that Simmons' vacated (to run against you). . . Plus, there's the referendum on your favorite issue of school finance. It should pass and most of those supporters like you. Getting a high turnout will be hard, but stranger things have happened. Remember, you won the lottery, and the Chicago Cubs won the division again this year. Luck seems to follow you," Kevin replies with a smile.

He then resumes speaking. "Win or lose Bob, you have nothing to be ashamed of. I assure you, (Senator) Simmons is a lot more nervous than we are tonight. HE is the one running against a political nobody. Rest assured, if the rumors about his drinking problem are true, he's on his third scotch right now. YOU are the one who the experts said had no chance to win. And Bob, regardless of what happens, you keep your head up high. But, please, go home and get some sleep. I'll be leaving as soon as I finish up some things," Kevin affirms as he and Bob exchange their goodbyes.

The alarm clock goes off at 4:00 a.m. The big day has arrived. Election Day. The day a political junkie lives for. Bob and his wife are up, but not yet gotten out of bed. Bob places his feet over the side of the bed as he slowly moves forward to start this important day. The digital clock reads 4:12 a.m. as he places his feet on the floor of the bedroom. He is seated on the edge of the bed and mumbles to himself, "It is time now. . . It's time to go." He gets up and proceeds to the bathroom.

Despite getting only four hours sleep, he feels great and surprisingly refreshed. He stares into the mirror and mumbles, "I need a miracle today. This campaign, which has been going fourteen months, will soon be over. Like Kevin said yesterday, anything can happen. Win or lose, God knows I've done my best," Bob states. He laughs after viewing himself in the mirror, gets dressed and eats breakfast with his wife. From the driveway she yells "Good luck Bob!! I love you a lot!!"

He returns to the front door, give his wife a big hug, and whispers "I love you too Trace. Thanks for everything the past year. I'll return at eight so we can go vote," Bob whispers. They hug each other tightly before he departs.

At 5:45 a.m. Bob arrives at the Calumet train station, located in Hazel Crest, Illinois. His three helpers John, Rick and Ken have not yet arrived. In the meantime, Bob begins to greet people, just as he had fourteen months before when the campaign started. He had campaigned at train stations more than forty times. By 7:30 a.m., he is a lot more cheerful. It appears that every fifth person he meets knows Bob personally. A few even stated that they have voted for him. His friends, working at the other entrance to the station, are getting similar replies from the commuters. "You know, Bob, we seem to be doing well. . . Everyone says they voted for you," Ken declares.

"Great news. . .But don't bet on it," Bob thinks while keeping his reply to himself. A key area from his discussion with Kevin the night before is very evident: the weather. There is no wind, the skies are blue, and the temperature is already 39 degrees, as indicated by the bank clock across the street.

"Things are okay guys, but I need to go and meet my wife. We are scheduled to vote between 8:00 and 8:30 this morning. All your help has been fantastic. I'll see you later today," Bob declares as he runs toward his car.

John yells out, "Bob, I think we are going to win today!!!"

The media sources wanted to take his photo while voting, but Bob did not want to delay anyone who was voting. It was decided to go after 8:00 when there would be fewer people there. About 8:40, Bob and Tracy arrive at Lincoln School. A group of ten or so members from the local media are waiting outside. As they approach the school, the cameras began clicking. They both smiled when a reporter from The Meteor asked "So Mr. Hamlin, is there anything you would like to state today?"

"Yes. I want to begin by thanking you all for coming today and to many previous events. This has been a long campaign with a lot of bitterness that has been shown by both sides. My wife, my staff, my supporters, and I appreciate your objectivity in reporting the facts over the past year. I hope everyone has a chance to come out and vote today. A democracy is only responsive when ALL our citizens participate in the electoral process. Regardless of who wins today, the most important fact to be stressed is that people exercise this right, which many have previously died to protect. For the elderly or those who have a harder time getting about, use the phone and ask someone to take you to the polls. Your vote is as important as mine," Bob states in an upbeat manner with a big smile on his face.

As the media entourage escorted Bob and Tracy inside the building, a middle- aged man recognized Bob from a previous campaign appearance. Bob had also visited his home when walking the neighborhood where he lived. To everyone's surprise, Bob recognized the humble man by saying, "Hello, Mr. Kropp. How are you today?"

"Hi Mr. Hamlin... I mean Bob," Mr. Andrew Kropp says, remembering what he had been told the day they sat down to talk. "Bob, I am so glad to vote. Things are not better at home. I'm still off work. . . I don't want to be critical, but Senator Simmons is a

151

class you know what. He's been in office for ten years and has done NOTHING. I cannot count the number of times I have called him asking for help," Mr. Kropp says as his voice cracks; he is trying to fight back the tears. "When you get a hold of him, he acts as if he has no clue what's happening. . .probably because he doesn't. I really hope you beat him!" Mr. Kropp shouts while shaking Bob's hand.

Mr. Kropp departs the building. The reporters look puzzled; partly because their view of Senator Simmons differed from his own, partly because a few noticed a tear forming in Bob Hamlin's eye.

"It is not Senator Simmons alone. Most people feel that our, and I do mean OUR, elected officials, don't care. The fear and anger within Mr. Kropp has been shown to me by thousands of people the past year. Afraid of losing their homes and fearful of what will become of their children's futures, I've met with countless people who told me they called Senator Simmons, many of them asking for help from the government..., most often for the first time in their lives. They called to ask for help. . .They told me they were turned away or taken for granted."

"People who have paid taxes and worked their entire lives, never asking for any handouts from the government, then to have that door shut in their faces. Anyone want to take a guess as to whose office they called?" Bob declares . . . "I solemnly assure each of you, if I win this election, people who need assistance on any matter - Social Security benefits to a student loan to getting their sidewalk fixed - people will learn that I can place them in the right direction to where they can get the help they need, the help they deserve. Today begins a new order." Bob states.

"Bob, why didn't you bring this up during the campaign?" a reporter from the Suburban Weekly asks.

"Was fearful I would be criticized for commenting on the constituent service record of the distinguished senator. . .I felt it would be best to let you see it for yourselves from a citizen in this district, not from me," Bob quietly says in response.

In many states there are laws pertaining to the distance people can campaign at an election site. In Illinois, the stated length is 100 feet, but oftentimes where you start measuring is where differences arise. One of the election judges felt that Bob was "campaigning" in the room where the polls were located. After being reminded about the law, Bob stated "thank you for reminding me. We are only here to cast our votes, then we are leaving. You are doing your job very well. Keep up the good work and have a nice day," Bob proclaims. He was polite, but she just did not want to hear anything he had to say.

After voting, Bob returns to the front table where the judges are. The woman was sitting there with her arms folded. She has been speaking the previous ten minutes on how "that damn young man had disturbed her election area and that no one was going to challenge her authority." Bob senses her anger at the situation and says, 'I'm terribly sorry if I upset you earlier. This has been a difficult campaign for everyone involved. I am sorry if you have been offended in any way," Bob states in a firm voice while extending his arm to shake hands.

Her arms still folded, she replies, "Well in that case, your apology is accepted." She never made eye contact with him. She was too busy looking over her shoulder, her thoughts someplace else. She was too ignorant to recognize Bob apologized only to ease the tension from the situation.

Two of the reporters present stopped to discuss what had just happened. One mentioned how Bob Hamlin had shown a lot of character by reaching out to apologize. The other, a female journalist who had covered local politics for 10 years said, "Yea. She was too proud to realize that his apology had nothing to do with her being correct because, as we saw, she was wrong. Maybe. . .we've underestimated Hamlin's strength of character."

Bob spends the rest of the day appearing on call-in shows, stopping by campaign offices of other local candidates, and making phone calls. On Election Day everyone tries to gauge voter turnout. Not only the total percentage, but in what geographic areas and what voter groups are participating in greater numbers. Shortly after 5:00 p.m. Bob arrives at the campaign office. It is buzzing with activity, with well over eighty people in the place.

As Bob and his wife Tracy open the door and walk in, everyone stops what they are doing. All the staff members and most of the volunteers proceed to applaud. Despite being overcome with happiness he too begins to clap in response. Many walk up to say hello and give him hugs. He greatly appreciates everyone's kindness but the person who Bob wants to speak with is Kevin. He notices Bob's arrival and quickly moves to get his attention. Upon reaching the rear of the office, they proceed to a room located beyond Kevin's desk.

Closing the door behind him, Kevin says, "Bob, I'm glad to see you. How you doing today?" The room is about three times the size of a closet, but it does permit some sense of privacy.

"I'm fine. It's been a long campaign, but I'm doing great. Believe me, I saw of lot of people in this campaign who are suffering from plant closings, health issues or some other pain and frustration, Bob replies

"Yea I know. I was yawning pretty hard about an hour ago, but I gained my second wind. Sometimes I yawn so hard it hurts my jaw. Are you ready for a long evening?" Kevin asks. His eyes are bloodshot, probably from the fact he had not slept the previous evening.

Any news on how things are going (with the voting turnout) since lunch?" Bob asks. They had not spoken since then.

"Well, I've got some good news. The (rate of voter) turnout is increasing. I know I mentioned earlier that things weren't going good. However, in many precincts randomly selected, the vote totals here are already higher than seen in the previous election two years ago.

The weather has got to be playing a role. Things are very strange. The turnout may approach what we would need to. We have a chance," Kevin whispers.

Later that night, Bob's friends and supporters gathered at a hotel in Matteson, Illinois, located right off Interstate 57. Throughout the evening, the crowd grew dramatically in size. Designed to seat about 200 people, it appeared as if the room was going to burst. It was decided to remove tables so more people could fit in the room, a move that would have upset the fire marshal had known what was happening. An overflow crowd of people had the luxury of some big screen TVs, a beautiful waterfall, and a great view within the interior of the hotel. Kevin kept Bob informed what was happening by telephone. They were located a few rooms apart on the second floor. Their rooms overlooked the lobby and restaurant area of the hotel. Occasionally, Bob could be seen in his room from the lobby. The audience would cheer upon seeing him.

As the time approached 11:30 p.m. it was still a dead heat. Bob was trailing by about 400 votes, but only 80 percent of the precincts had reported. Shortly before midnight, Bob was called to the telephone. Kevin had spent the previous few moments speaking with Jim Hanson, a local political operative in Will County. The district extended through five counties in Illinois. It had an odd looking shape. In fact, it looked like a salamander. Its people had very diverse ethnic backgrounds, a variety of income levels, etc. would complicate the problems any candidate would face, let alone a 25-year-old newcomer such as Bob Hamlin.

"Bob!" Kevin shouted from across the room, waving his finger indicating he wanted him to come over. "Bob, I need to speak with you again. . . alone. This way you can hear for yourself what is happening," Kevin requested.

After going into a private room, Bob answered the call.

"Yes, Mr. Hanson. How are you today?... Good. Thanks for asking. What's happening out there?" Bob politely asks.

"Well Bob, as usual we have had our typical problem with the polling machines out here. That partly explains the reason you do not know the results yet. I felt you were owed a courtesy call to inform you of the news before you hear from anyone else. You have lost the Will County portion of your district by only 388 votes. Considering the fact your opponent is a local powerhouse out here and had to collect on a lot. . . and I mean A LOT of IOU's What you've done is near miraculous. If your opponent were anyone else today, anyone short of the Lord, you would have won Will County. I, myself, thought you would lose out here by 1400 votes. . . Win or lose, you should be very proud of yourself son," Mr. Hanson proclaims in a positive, mature manner.

"Thank you very much for the news sir. Your help these past few months has been fantastic," Bob replies in a sad tone.

"Don't be sad. You've done great. Kevin tells me...you may have a chance. And you'll do so knowing you did it the right way: by telling the truth. I really hope you win. In losing by only 388 votes out in this part of the district, you're gonna win. The senator puts on a good show, but he's really an SOB. . . You know, (Senator) Simmons is living proof that most humans use only one quarter of their brain capacity," Mr. Hanson says as Bob breaks out in laughter, dropping the phone on the ground. He continues to laugh uncontrollably for five minutes.

Chapter Eighteen
Winning Is Only Part of the Game in Politics

Shortly before 1:45 a.m. Kevin approaches the podium. "To make a long story short, and in recognition that this has been a very long evening, I am pleased to introduce to you all the newest Congressman from the 4th District of Illinois, my friend and yours, MR. ROBERT HAMLIN!!!!" Kevin shouts.

The 120 or so people who remained erupted in happiness. The noise and level of emotion climbs by the second as the crowd jumps, cheers, and hugs each other, whether they know each other or not. Bob, after hugging his wife, approaches his friend Kevin and gives him a huge embrace, lasting more than one minute in length. After what seemed like forever, Bob turns to face the faithful who were still present.

"Thank you!!!" Bob shouts as the crowd roars again. Many in attendance are crying from their happiness for the victory that is now at hand. Some of them had given more than 300 hours of their free time during the previous year. They now notice that Bob himself has tears rolling down the side of his face.

"Thank you. Thank you Thank you!" Bob states to the crowd. "I will probably have a hard time talking. My voice is shot and. . ." Bob whispers. He realizes the difficulty in speaking because he is overcome with emotion. After a few seconds, the crowd proudly responds to the situation by chanting his last name. "Hamlin, Hamlin, Hamlin!!"

Bob wipes the tears away and says, "It has been a long day for everyone. I will keep this very, very, very short" as the crowd begins to laugh, after growing used to his long emotional speeches during the campaign.

"Almost fifteen minutes ago I received a phone call from Senator Michael Simmons. We spoke for about three minutes regarding today's events and the campaign in general. He called to offer his congratulations on our win today. He was very kind and polite and his tone was sincere. . .It's been a difficult and stressful campaign for all parties involved. Senator Simmons has graciously offered to throw a 'Breakfast for Reconciliation' a week from today. He's extending an olive branch for success, hope, and goodwill for the residents of the Fourth District - so that we may all move forward. I want to publicly thank Senator Simmons for being so gracious in defeat," Bob affirms to the applause of the crowd.

"I have. . .too many people to thank. So as not to forget anyone, I want to begin by thanking everyone, particularly you all who are still here at nearly 2:00 a.m." Bob says while looking at his watch. The crowed cheers wildly for ten seconds, then Bob resumes his speech.

"I want to thank my parents. Regardless of how stubborn and impatient I've been, they have ALWAYS been there for me. I'm just a branch that has grown from a very solid tree," Bob says as the crowd applauds to recognize Bob's parents, both of whom are still in attendance.

"Also, I want to thank my friend Kevin. Throughout the campaign, I was advised, some would say TOLD, to hire a more seasoned campaign manager. I initially asked Kevin because I knew he was fantastic at making people feel good and feeling as if they are a key part of the team. He's so polite he almost makes people feel guilty when they were not helping our campaign. We stuck with you and you gave us a win. . . Thanks," Bob states as the crowd cheers loudly. Bob and Kevin publicly show their friendship by giving each other another long embrace.

"Last, I want to thank my wife. She has seen me at my best and at my worst. Through it all, she's been as kind as the day I first met her. She not only is my wife but, more importantly, my best friend. Tracy, I love you," Bob whispers as the crowd explodes, showing their happiness. Kevin leads those present by chanting her name. For about eight seconds, nearly 100 people all yell her name. "Tracy, Tracy, Tracy, Tracy."

"Once again, I want to thank you all. Drive home safely so we can all gather again soon. Wish I had more to say, but I feel we should all go home and get some sleep. In four hours I will be doing what was done as we began our campaign: greeting the people the citizens of this district at the train station. Anyone want to join me?" Bob asks as the crowd moans. A few boos are even heard.

"Oh well, that's OK. Thank you. May God bless you all," Bob states as the crowd erupts in happiness.

"Good afternoon, Congressman Hamlin's office. . . Yes, Congressman Hamlin will be speaking tomorrow morning before the seniors' organization in Homewood at 10:00 a.m.. . . Yes, anyone can attend. There is no charge for the event. . . There is ample parking and refreshments will be available. . . Are there any other questions you may have? Thank you for calling Congressman Hamlin's office. . . Bye," Miss Sharon Perry states. She decided to join the staff upon Bob Hamlin's offer shortly after the election. Sharon works out of the district office in Chicago Heights, Illinois.

The final tally showed Bob Hamlin won the election by 462 votes. A brief recount of 25 percent of the district's precincts showed his margin of victory had actually increased. Senator Simmons publicly announced that he was canceling all future challenges to the electoral results. Despite the personal differences he and Bob had during the campaign, they had sat down and talked at least three times after the election. Senator Simmons was very helpful in advising Bob how to open district offices, hiring staff people, and responding to constituent issues. Odd, because the whole time he was not stopping any effort to challenge the fact that Bob Hamlin won the election.

It is now March. Bob Hamlin has been in office for two months now. Despite winning four months ago, the pace and schedule of events have not slowed down at all. Bob's time was in constant demand. Interest groups would hold fundraising and "Let's get acquainted" activities. Bob attended as many events as was humanly possible. To no one's surprise, the group where he did the worst in the last election was with those people age 60 and over. Bob had conceded often that in speeches before senior citizens groups, he understood the lack of trust that existed between them. Unlike other politicians who may avoid potentially hostile audiences, Bob ran toward them. "To overcome their doubts, I will have to meet with senior citizens as often as possible. After all, if we fail, it will only prove that they were right about me: that a young person is not willing to address their concerns because they do not understand," Bob declared in a staff meeting. He instructed his staff to do EVERYTHING within their power to create a line of communication between Bob and the older citizens in his district.

It would be fair to say that the opposition took Bob Hamlin too lightly this past time. A Republican had represented the district in the U.S. Congress for the past fifty years. Therefore, despite his money, Bob was never given any serious consideration of winning. Defeating a well-known scandal-free incumbent state senator was never expected, even over an open or 'vacant' seat. "Letting Mr. Hamlin win was a mistake neither we nor anyone will ever allow to happen again," an advisor for the Republican Congressional Campaign Committee had privately stated.

When told of the quote, Bob privately stated "Hey, if I were them, I would be upset too. However, we won this election by addressing the issues and the needs of the people who live here, not what some (political) consultant in Washington DC felt would politically help me. The voters spoke and we heard them," Bob declared.

And listen Bob did. A local state representative sat down with Bob and explained the situation to him. "To be reelected will require you to campaign constantly. It will be as if we lost and are running again. You are in great shape and have an endless supply of energy. The people elected you; now you have the responsibility of serving the citizens here to the best of your abilities."

Bob Hamlin even welcomed the challenge. "Anyone wanting to win back this seat is going to have to work three times as hard as us. . . that may not be physically possible," Bob stated with a smile to his closest staff and political consultants.

Arriving early for the big event before the senior citizens, Bob greeted each person with a firm handshake, looked into their eyes, and repeated each person's name as they entered the room. "You may not be perfect, but you always try to make people feel good about them," a member of the Glenwood Senior Citizens Club once told him.

Bob began his speech by acknowledging the presence of those in the crowd who he knew. After fifteen minutes, he noticed he was starting to lose the attention of the crowd. He then decided to try something very unusual.

"You know, sometimes speeches are just too long. Many times, you soon find them to be boring. This may seem unusual, but I am going to ask everyone to stand," Bob states. He jumps down off the podium and leads the people in a series of exercises. At first the 200 plus people in attendance were very hesitant to play along. But after Bob kept at it, he soon had most of the people moving around at their seats. Four minutes after leaving the podium, he returned to continue his speech. Some were shaking their heads and asking each other questions about where this 26-year-old person was coming from.

"I want to be perfectly clear. I fully understand that I was not the favorite to win last fall. I also know that I did not fare well among your age group. I called this meeting to let you know that I am here for you. The issues you care about are the issues I will be facing each day as a Congressman."

"This does not mean that we will always get along or agree on everything. I believe that the Social Security System needs to be modified. NO ONE is arguing to eliminate the system. The program was created as a safety net for older Americans to supplement their private retirement plans. It was NOT made to be used as a source of funding for vacations and tours by wealthier Americans," Bob stated. Among the crowd is a large chorus of boos. The crowd's reply did not surprise Bob in the slightest.

"I understand your willingness to disagree. You see, now we're communicating," Bob says while walking away from the podium. He begins to walk among the crowd. "We will have differences on some key issues."

"I do not intend to run away from anyone. Permit me to tell you what else I feel is important. I will push hard to make prescription drugs more affordable. I will work, not just vote, for changes in our health care system to provide EVERYONE, regardless of age and wealth, the access to basic care. I will help to RAISE, not cut, the monthly benefits of most Social Security recipients - so that no retired American has to eat dog food. Health care should be made a fundamental right, not a benefit for the wealthy. And most importantly, I will work for passage of a catastrophic health care plan. American families should not be forced to hide assets to qualify as being poor. If every defendant has the right to legal counsel, every American should have some level of access to better health care," Bob says. The crowd responds wildly with positive cheers and applause. In fact, many of the poorer retirees present stand up to show their support for Bob's statement—much to the dismay of some retirees present who were wealthier.

Seventeen months later in October, Bob was facing another difficult reelection fight against Senator Simmons. At first, the senator had been helpful and had assisted Bob in establishing an office. However, over the past few months his detractors referred to the fact that being defeated by a "nobody," as Bob Hamlin, wounded his pride. This injury to his pride was stronger than his willingness to serve the general public. Even some of the senator's supporters now turned on him because it provided an example of what the senator's critics stated all along: "His head (ego) is larger than his heart," as one critic was quoted as saying. Various campaign committees, making the option of taking another chance to defeat Bob Hamlin easier, promised Simmons to finance his campaign.

Senator Al Howard of Louisiana was scheduled to be the main speaker at Bob's fundraiser. At $250 per ticket, the goal was to raise $25,000 for the next month. Al Howard had represented Louisiana as a U.S. Senator for the previous twelve years. Always considered a potential presidential candidate, he was very successful in raising money for other Democratic candidates across the nation. Bob had known of Senator Howard for at least the previous six years and had studied his record of achievements. To be blunt, Bob "worshipped" Senator Howard: He was kind of like his political hero. Having him come to Illinois to aid his reelection effort made Bob feel very honored. Being 62 years of age, it was rumored Senator Howard would run for the presidency in the next election, which was scheduled to occur two years from now.

Reasons for agreeing to come to Chicago to help Bob's reelection varied. He was not well known in the state of Illinois. Coming would increase his exposure to wealthy contributors who primarily finance presidential campaigns. Also, it allowed him to secure an early endorsement for the presidency from the youngest member of Congress and meet other key elected officials in this Midwest state. Primarily, however, Senator Howard liked Bob personally. They had jointly sponsored legislation to reform the student loan system. He viewed Bob as studious, hard working, and quiet - almost a much younger version of himself. "I just wish Bob Hamlin was fifteen years older," Senator Howard had privately confessed to one of his own supporters.

After being introduced, Senator Howard was warmly received with a standing ovation. Only forty percent (if that) of the crowd knew who he was. Nevertheless, he stood before them and proudly stated, "I am here to show my support for the reelection of Robert Hamlin to the U.S. Congress. There are many problems still facing America despite how hard Bob Hamlin has worked the previous two years. When I first met Bob, I honestly thought he was a lobbyist. Good looking, well dressed. . . probably had a lot of money, was how I viewed him at the time. Imagine my surprise when I was told he was a member of the Congress. . . that's the other body of government you know. I asked myself why such a fine person would want to be here." Senator Howard said, drawing laughs from the crowd.

"What I learned is what you'll knew. He's a fine man with good roots (pronounced like ROOTs) and a strong backbone," Senator Howard declared in a deep southern accent.

"I was born and raised in Baton Rouge, Louisiana. I won't state my age, but Bob Hamlin is about half mine. My parents taught me a long time ago about character: respect for others, honesty, care, and concern. There are very few people in the U.S. Congress like him, him being too young and all for the job," Senator Howard says, drawing laughter from the crowd, "who enjoy the respect Robert Hamlin has earned. We need more people in Congress who are like him!" Senator Howard shouts, prompting a standing ovation from the crowd.

"It is my firm belief that the best speech in politics is one that is short. My pappy used to tell me that 'the mind cannot absorb what the rump cannot endure' (bringing laughter from the crowd). I know that long speeches are boring, so I gave 'em up a long time ago. Mr.

Hamlin, after hearing your three previous speeches on the House floor, you'd be surprised how helpful that advice can be," Senator Howard declares after turning toward Bob, causing him to pause briefly while looking at Bob. The crowd is amused with Howard's comments and continues to laugh.

"Mr. Hamlin, I have successfully run for office for the past thirty years without a loss. Sometimes the best speakers are recognized as such for being good listeners. . . If you watch one of your own speeches, you'd know what I mean," Senator Howard says with a smile as the crowd continues laughing.

"These young know-it-alls: you know who they are. . . On a serious note, I am proud to be here tonight. Robert Hamlin is a good person with a fine future ahead of him. He seems to have that SPECIAL knack to help people: regardless of their wealth or political pull. You wanted him, now you have him. If I were his mama, I'd be proud of him too. It gives me great pleasure to introduce to you Mr. Robert Hamlin!" Senator Howard declares while turning again toward the young man.

The audience consisting of nearly 800 people all stand as Bob approaches the podium and shakes the Senator's hand. Both smile from the visible sign of mutual admiration. Few people at the time could imagine the two having a future together.

After a minute of applause, Bob addresses the crowd.

"Senator Howard, thank you for that very kind introduction. I hope and pray you will run for the presidency two years from now. We need you. . . AMERICA needs you!" Bob declares in a firm voice as the crowd rises to applaud.

"The issues Senator Howard and I have worked for are the struggles that the people of America face on a daily basis. I keep bringing up the issues of our schools, crime, the future, etc. because the problems don't just go away and they don't become fixed by themselves. The legislation to tackle these problems is held up in the U.S. Congress. We need. . . " Bob states as he continues with his speech.

After the dust settles, Bob Hamlin is reelected with a winning margin of 54 - 46 percent. His presence in the U.S. Congress representing the South Suburbs will remain as long as he and the voters now want. "Despite all the talk about "throwing out the bums," defeating an incumbent is very difficult, particularly a young man like Hamlin who really does care," says John Ormsby, Mayor of Calumet City, Illinois.

As a 28-year-old member of Congress his talents are in strong demand. He could run for the U.S. Senate two years from now, join the board of a major corporation, etc. Instead he decides to run for reelection again and volunteer as a member of the steering committee for the "Fund for a Strong Future," the Political Action Committee or PAC of Senator Al Howard. Now 63, Senator Howard has agreed to run for the presidency. In explaining his decision to his home state supporters, he says, "I have done my best to represent Louisiana. The time to offer America the level of leadership which this nation used to have has now come."

Since Bob has spent a lot of time giving speeches and meeting as many people as he can, his voting attendance record is much lower than it should be. Unlike the perception the American people have for how other elected officials act, Bob does feel a sense of guilt. He was constantly criticized by his detractors for missing votes; much of it the past year when he actually toured the district with Senator Simmons, his former opponent from two prior campaigns.

When asked by a local reporter whether he expected any potential opponents, he replied, "We fully expect to see two to three people who will run. EVERYONE can. After all, no one thought we had a chance to win in our first campaign. However, we will continue to work, work, and work on the issues that still confront us. The people of this district and the needs faced by all our communities throughout the Chicagoland area and the rest of the state of Illinois are too great to ignore."

Later, another reporter asked Bob about his support for Senator Howard's presidential campaign. He was asked if any "promises" were made. Bob's reply was unusually strong: "I have been an admirer of Senator Howard for the past eight years. I support him because he, oftentimes by himself, leads the effort to fight for the issues that I care most about. I intend to work for him and hope I have the honor to campaign with him," Bob responded. The same reporter then stated, "As a follow up question, you recall they changed the U.S. Constitution seven years ago." It was done when Bob Hamlin was in college. It removed the age requirement to run for federal offices, including the presidency. "Is there any truth to the rumor that you are being considered as a running mate for Senator Howard?"

Bob starts to laugh. After a few brief seconds, he replies to the question. "I normally pay close attention to the rumor mill regarding the field of politics. I myself have not heard that one yet. . .I'm truly sorry. But, where did you hear that?" Bob asks. He truly was surprised as the question, for he had not contemplated the issue.

Bob then departs to return to the office. He dismissed what was just said by remembering why he entered politics in the first place: "To use government as a means to resolve others' problems and to enable people to help themselves to better their lives, regardless of their financial situation," Bob stated while thinking to himself.

Entering his office, Sharon Perry is rather excited. "Bob, you received many calls today. However, there is one in particular you should return first," she states.

"Is it my wife? Did she call?" Bob questions.

"Yea, she did, but Senator Al Howard called today. He said it was important," she responds.

After first calling his wife to see how she's doing, Bob returns the phone call to Senator Howard. Their conversation lasts for approximately fifteen minutes.

"Bob, it's a go. We're full steam ahead. I'm going to run. The official announcement will be in September," the senator revealed. "How would you like to spend an entire day around Chicago to campaign with me? You can set up the entire schedule as you wish. How does that sound?" Senator Howard asks in a deep southern accent.

"It would be an honor to sir. I will GLADLY do as you wish to help you. Don't need to ask for my endorsement. You have it sir," Bob replies.

One month later the big day came. His entire staff was used to prepare the schedule. It began with a breakfast with local union leaders. Being from a southern state, union members doubted his commitment to support laws for job safety and legislation to protect working people. Before 12 Noon, Howard and Hamlin met with the editorial boards of the two major newspapers. At 2:00 p.m. a press conference was held. This allowed the media to ask specific questions and made their job easier in preparing a story for the evening news broadcast. He came across as calm, mature, effective and friendly - just as Bob Hamlin had viewed him many times in the past.

Shortly before 5:00 p.m., Senator Howard visited a local day care center. It allowed him to touch base with a group of "very young people," born two generations after him. From an image standpoint it was a huge success. Senator Howard came across as a very caring grandfather. But more importantly, he was convinced that a greater effort was needed by the federal government to help families requiring day care for their children.

Later that evening a huge dinner was held in Senator Howard's honor at the same hotel in Matteson, Illinois, where Bob celebrated his first victory. Everyone who gave money or his or her time to Bob's campaign was invited. A charge of only $10 was asked to help cover expense for the event.

"Our intent is not to raise money. The objective is to meet a great human being who has done so much for this nation. I hope you can come," Robert Hamlin wrote in the invitation that was distributed.

And come they did. Additional parking lots were reserved with bus service to shuttle the crowd to the event. For those in attendance, estimated at 1,500 people, there were not enough seats for everyone. Many came to show their appreciation to Bob for his service in Congress. Others came because they wanted to hear and meet someone who Bob had frequently quoted in his speeches.

"I am sorry that everyone cannot see or hear me this evening. But I assure you, I will return in the future," Senator Howard offered.

"And that is what this race is all about, the future of this country It concerns the ability of our children to meet the challenge facing us from overseas so we can continue to compete in the world marketplace. If we are successful, we can continue to provide for a future we can all be proud of. For those of you in your 40's, please listen. The investment we make today to educate our kids will be seen by people earning higher wages in the future - providing for Social Security income to protect your retirement. It is well documented how economic growth came in the 1950's because we educated our veterans from World War II. It was no accident. It was a result of an investment in us," Howard declared. Many seniors rose to their feet to applaud, for they were old enough to remember what he was talking about.

"Next year's election will be very important. Regardless of who wins, there is much work to be done. Under the current administration nothing is being done. Our present method of staying the course does nothing to provide a better future for our nation. When you change NOTHING, one result is that no one will get upset. The path of change is a difficult course. Many interests will be threatened. A lot of money will be spent trying to defeat Bob Hamlin and me in our individual political careers. What is important are the beliefs and issues we hold closest to us. Regardless of the obstacles we face, we must push ahead. The costs of doing nothing far exceed the errors of continuing on the present path."

"I notice many of you, particularly our senior citizens present, applauding frequently. You must like what y'all hear, right?" Senator Howard says. "Why then is my boy Hamlin here having such difficulty with you'll?" he says in a deep southern accent. "He says the same things I do, yet his poll numbers are low. . . If you can applaud happily for me - why not for my young friend, Mr. Hamlin?" Howard declares, as the crowd rises to its feet as a visible show of support for Hamlin's legislative efforts.

"I ask you to join us in our quest for our nation with a better future. We live in the greatest country in the history of the world, but we are not perfect. Don't be fooled by pride or 30-second campaign commercials. We do have our faults. The best hitter in baseball is lucky to hit .350. He is unsuccessful two of every three at bats. We as a nation, much like a batting champion, can still be even better."

"I want to thank you for your time and presence here tonight. Just because we do not see each other every month does not mean we are far apart. I will continue to fight for what I believe in. All I ask is that you study the issues, and ask yourselves the following question: Have we left our nation in good hands for our children? After searching your heart if you provide the answer is no, then join with us. There are good people in the U.S. Congress, like Robert Hamlin, who need your help. Thanks. May the good Lord keep watch over you and protect you," Senator Howard declares to the cheering crowd. Many stay afterwards for the chance to have a photo taken or shake his hand.

One year later, Senator Howard was campaigning full speed ahead. He had won most of the "Super Tuesday" states and had even won the Illinois Democratic primary. He was well on his way toward winning the nomination for his party to run for president. All that stood between him and the nomination was winning the California primary. The only key issue facing both Senator Howard and the party was who would be chosen as a running mate. Rumors were flying everywhere about this and that senator. For Senator Al Howard, picking a running mate was a responsibility he did not take lightly, especially over the previous three months as he won more Democratic primaries and caucuses.

He wanted someone who he could trust and rely on, if something unfortunate were to happen to him. But, he also wanted a person who he felt comfortable with. Decision time was soon drawing near.

Chapter Nineteen
Don't Be Afraid To Take a Chance

Senator Al Howard was on his way to winning the presidential nomination. However, it did not prevent others from passing up the chance to give advice. Every senator and political "spin doctor" had an opinion as to who should be selected as his running mate. Calls from around the country came in to Baton Rouge, Louisiana, the national headquarters of the Howard for President Campaign. Visitors flew in as well. They included registered lobbyists, labor union leaders, members of Congress, and key party officials. There was no consensus among the various groups as to who should be chosen. The potential candidates were of all ages, ethnic, and political backgrounds.

Many of the people mentioned by the "experts" had been in office a long time. The key interest and constituent groups who came before Senator Howard in Louisiana frequently mentioned these people. Howard came to question whether they really wanted to win the presidential election by recommending someone who best suited their (typically losing) political philosophy. After all, not all of the people or groups giving their opinions supported him in his campaign bid. In fact, many helped other candidates in the various Democratic primaries. Regardless of why they came, Senator Howard did extend each the courtesy to convey their particular message. "After all, my mother did not raise no dummy," Senator Howard was jokingly quoted when asked to explain his longevity in politics. In the end, he knew he would need the support of everyone to win.

One particular visitor caught Senator Howard by surprise: Senator James Collins from Massachusetts. He had been in office for nearly sixteen years now and had co-sponsored numerous pieces of legislation with Senator Howard over the years. His pick for a running mate caught Howard by complete surprise. "Why don't you pick the kid? You know, the young man from Illinois," Collins asked.

"Whom are you referring to?" Howard naively asked.

"Representative Hamlin from Illinois," Collins responded in a firm voice.

"You and I have been in this body (the U.S. Senate) a long time. How could you even consider Hamlin? Don't get me wrong. He is very astute, a tireless worker, and a fine young man. But let's be realistic. He's what. . . 28 or 29 years old?" Senator Howard questions in a loud voice. "He's too young." Howard shouts in response. When the Constitution was amended eight years before, it prohibited discrimination in hiring by age. It was designed to protect older workers from being displaced. Therefore, the age requirement had been removed.

"Now Al, I know it seems like it's hopeless, but consider the facts first. He's only 29, but hear me out. You are losing in our polls by eighteen percentage points. As it stands now, with the economy really not being that bad, you're going to lose. You are eight years older than (President Joseph) Crowe. Therefore, I think you should pick someone much younger as a running mate. The senior citizens know and respect your record. What better way to show how serious you are about the future than by picking someone who represents the future? You're down now, why not take a chance by picking him?" Collins asks, trying to be reasonable. However, Howard's patience was being tested.

"I've been here too long and worked too hard to end my political career getting destroyed by choosing him as my running mate!! You want me to end my Senate career doing what. . . getting killed in this election?" Senator Howard asks.

"You're losing bad now and Hamlin's not on the ticket. I know it seems odd but think about it. The economy is not that bad and we're not at war with anyone. To defeat President Crowe you will have to convince the voters that this election is about the future. America will become stronger if we make the needed changes now. . . What better way to show how serious you are by picking a running mate from another generation? I know Congressman Hamlin is not the best choice, but doing what is safe will only bring you defeat this fall. Al, I've known you a long time. I'm only trying to be honest with you," Collins says as he placed his hand on Howard's shoulder. "I owe you nothing less than the truth."

"Jim, I like Hamlin. Believe me, I really do. We have spent three days together over the past fourteen months. He is honest, bright. . .good looking, and loyal. Someday he will be a great candidate for this office. I really feel that choosing him now would be rushing his career and decreasing our chances to win. However, I do value your opinion. After all, we've won on legislation with shorter odds than Hamlin. There have been a lot of the members of Congress and lobbyists here giving their opinion. I really like Bob Hamlin. . .Two or three other people have named him too," Senator Howard mumbles.

"You mean I am not the only one to bring HIM up!" Senator Collins shouts, his tone suddenly turning hostile.

"I'm sorry I did not mention it. I only want to hear input from as many sources as possible, without revealing that said what and why. It's only fair to everyone," Senator Howard responds.

"We've known each other nearly twenty years. I'm sure that you have considered me as a possible running mate," Collins suggests.

"That's correct. Several people, in fact, have suggested you as the running mate. Believe me, I've got no qualms picking you. I have given the topic serious thought," Howard replies.

"Picking me would mean you would listen to my advice and trust my judgment, would it not?" Senator Collins inquires.

"Yes. I view you as family. We've worked together very well," Howard replies.

"Good, then listen to me. I'm offering Hamlin's name for consideration. He's very intelligent, much more mature than we would expect from someone his age. He spends a great deal of time documenting his research to show the validity of his arguments. The passion he demonstrates on key issues like education and planning for the future warrant a lot of respect. Hell, even the Republicans like him. Look at the district he won in. I was told that there is NO way a Democrat should win in his district, let alone a 25-year-old who has no military background... He won and continues to win because he's good at what he does. . . He genuinely loves working with and helping people."

"I have read about our young Hamlin. His story is remarkable. . . He wins the lottery. Instead of spending the money pleasing himself, who most people would do if they won, he finishes college. Despite doing well, he later drops out of law school after one year and starts a business. He donates a lot of his own money to charity and helps raise more money from others. He marries his girlfriend from college,"

"Later he runs for Congress in a district that even I would not run in, then wins. Gets reelected and continually impresses most members of Congress, even though he is half their age. When he first arrived here, he was upsetting people by doing things like sponsoring bills to make defeating incumbents easier. Now, everyone respects him. It shows he's willing to listen and learn," Senator Collins states, shaking his head almost in disbelief.

"Why do you think that is? What's so special about him? What's the magic?" Senator Howard asks.

"Well, it's no spell. I really believe he understands how things work and what makes people tick. He constantly works trying to meet the needs of the people whom he represents. He was advised that he was too critical of his fellow House members. So what does he do? He shuts up. He sat down and took his seat in the chamber. Hell, how many people in Washington do you know who keep quiet when they are asked to do so?" Collins asks. Howard responds by shrugging his shoulders and throwing his arms up in the air.

"He attends all committee meetings, while keeping his mouth shut. Instead of working against Congress, he now works within the rules to get things done. As a result, he is more effective at getting legislation passed and his popularity among the members is much higher now. He has learned how things get done. . . Who better to lobby the Congress as a vice president?" Senator Collins offers.

"Tell you what. . .I'll consider what you've have said today. However, I will also consider what others have said about their choices. I also want you to consider being my running mate. When I've made my final decision, I'll let you know. This race is TOO important for the future of this nation. Perhaps Hamlin would be a good president. However, I will only choose a running mate who will serve to help my campaign, not endanger it. Thanks for your input. I'm sorry for how I responded," Senator Howard states.

"No, thank you for listening. But take my name off the list. You don't need a liberal from the Northeast on the ticket. You need Hamlin," Collins replies.

"If you were in my position, who would you pick?" Howard inquires.

"I've been telling you for the past twenty minutes. Pick him," Collins answers in an upbeat manner.

Both men stand and exchange handshakes as Senator Collins is escorted to the exit. The level of Secret Service protection is remarkably high, not that any particular threat to Howard's life is present.

After weighing all the advice he has received, Howard narrows his choice to three possible candidates. Two weeks remain before the start of the Democratic convention. Howard himself had set a deadline for choosing a running mate to one week before hand. Two of the finalists are established and nationally known members of Congress: one a senator from Ohio and the other the House Majority Leader from Minnesota. However, with most voters in an uproar from long-term congressional service and the continual stories about the documented abuses of power, perhaps picking someone with fewer years of service would not be a bad idea. Both had been in the U.S. Congress more than 16 years. Senator Al Howard had 18 years' experience in the Senate, not including six years 6 as a member of the U.S. House of Representatives. After much lobbying from numerous interest groups and political party activists, Howard finalizes his decision.

The announcement would be revealed in five days before the start of the convention, which was scheduled for the following Monday. Three sessions with the media were planned during Thursday and Friday. The first was scheduled for Baton Rouge, Louisiana, Thursday morning. The second session would be on Thursday afternoon in Los Angeles, whose state had the largest number of electoral votes. The third was planned for Chicago, Illinois, site of the convention on Friday afternoon. Much to the surprise of everyone, except his wife and Senator Collins, Senator Howard had decided on picking 29-year-old U.S. Representative Robert Hamlin from Illinois as his running mate.

The "call" was placed Tuesday afternoon. After a two-hour discussion, Robert Hamlin accepted the offer to run as Senator Howard's vice presidential candidate. The decision to accept was very difficult. Bob was notified by a close source that he was under consideration, but never considered himself a finalist. In fact, he was flattered, but didn't give the topic any more thought. He, himself, nominated Senator Collins for the position when he spoke with Senator Howard about the issue. In fact, all the negatives about Bob brought by everyone, including Bob himself, were discussed. Despite the perception held by a few people that he was "begging" for the position, the truth was he lobbied strongly against himself or anyone young like him.

However, Senator Howard would have none of it. "Bob, I picked you and your age as an asset - not to be a knock against you. I too expressed the same opinion when Senator Jim Collins of Massachusetts named you. He and I came to the Senate a long time ago. . . He argued forcefully that you could help me. Your work habits, knowledge of the issues, and your background will help me in my campaign, he argued. Believe me, I had the same doubts about you that you are expressing yourself. However, I trust and value his and other people's judgement. A leader makes decisions after weighing the facts and then sticks to them. Bob, I've made my decision. I'm asking you to be my running mate," Senator Howard declared. A listener could easily identify his deep accent.

"I am truly shocked Senator, but if you feel I can best help you in this capacity, I will honor your request," Hamlin states after declining the offer two hours before. "I will gladly run with you, go where you want me to go, and do what you and the campaign staff want done. I'll work and be a team player. Whatever it takes, I'm at your service," Hamlin explained.

"Great to hear Son! We will announce our decision Thursday morning. If you and your wife can come, my wife Lillian and I would be honored to have you as our guests' tomorrow evening. That way, I know you will not be late the following day," Senator Howard replies as they both laugh.

"Senator, I have one major problem. How do I tell my wife the news? It's safe to say she will not be happy," Bob states in a somber voice.

"My friend, go tell your wife now. If this is something she does not want to do, call me tonight and I'll ask someone else tomorrow. If she hesitates, call me and we'll work together with no regrets. Lillian and I have been married a long time. . .She's a lot stronger person than she is perceived on TV. We're the best of friends and we run for office together. One cannot operate without the other. Do you understand Bob?" Senator Howard asks.

"Yes sir, I do. Either way, I'll call tonight," Bob replies.

The topic of running for the vice presidency had been briefly brought up once before in Tracy's presence. However, she dismissed the idea as fiction. The subject was then not discussed because both felt no need to talk about what would never happen. She objected to Bob's candidacy for anything, let alone the U.S. Congress, for her opposition to and boredom with politics. Now her husband, only 29 years old, was scheduled to be the Democratic Nominee for Vice President.

"Bob, what are you doing? Bob what are WE doing? I've given up a lot being the wife of a Congressman for you. You'll be traveling across the whole nation! You will be away much more often. And what about us!!! This was not on the agenda!!!" Tracy asked, her emotions now getting the best of her.

"I know how you feel. You deserve someone who is here more than I. Senator Howard is a great person. Someone whose leadership the country needs," Bob responds as she cuts him off.

"Great Person for the nation?" Tracy says, flabbergasted. "This is not one of your press conferences. What about us Bob? Did you forget I hate politics? I am ONLY involved because I love and respect you, not the GAME known as politics!" Tracy replies while shouting at Bob.

"Tracy, if you really do not want this now, tell me again. If you like I'll call Senator Howard back right NOW, not next week, to decline the offer. I'm serious, if that's what you want, then let's do it. It's not too late for anything: not the campaign and not our marriage. But if that is what you really want, we have to call him now," Bob replies. After a few moments he continues speaking, much more calmly "I told him yes, but it does not mean the decision is etched in stone. I conveyed to him that my acceptance would be contingent on your support and he agreed. We have not signed on the dotted line," Bob proclaims.

Needless to say, his wife is surprised. "You really would do that for me?" Tracy asks. After all, it was the first time Bob had declined anything politically the past four years. "You are serious? For the first time, ever, I sense your sincerity about not running. I'd thought I would never see the day."

"Tracy, I married you, not the political system," Bob states. After a long period of hugging each other, they end their embrace. Her statement then really surprised him.

"Come on. We have to go upstairs and pack. We have a few trips this week," Tracy explains with a smile as a tear rolls down her cheek.

"Are you sure? Remember, we have our whole life ahead of us to do this," Bob inquires.

"No we don't. This opportunity only comes once in a lifetime. Besides, if you win, it will mean your political career will end sooner, right?" Tracy asks.

They both laugh hard and give each another long hug.

"Tracy, I love you," Bob says.

Tracy releases Bob and replies, "I know you do, and that's why I am letting you run again. Win or lose, this will be our last campaign together. No more Bob. We need to spend more time together. Who knows how long we'll both be here. God willing, I hope you win so we can get on with the rest of our lives. Make no mistake about what I said. This is it. No more Congress. No Governor's race. After this election we start to have a family. You'll be there one term and then we're getting out of politics. You can become a lobbyist: You can work half as hard and earn twice as much. I now know how this works. Do you understand me? No more. This is our last election together. Make no mistake about this. That is a statement, not a question," Tracy says. The look on her face clearly reveals there will be no misunderstanding.

177

"Yes I do. For the first time, I do," Bob responds. "One election. Four more years and that's it. I promise you that." They both give each other a long embrace.

On Thursday morning, the two couples, joined by about 100 Secret Service personnel, are at a hotel in Baton Rouge, Louisiana. At the podium the Howards and Hamlins are joined by more than thirty members of Congress and most of the political leadership from the state of Louisiana. After everyone is situated, Senator Howard approaches the microphone.

"I want to thank all of you for coming today. This race is about the future of our nation. Many challenges await us and the solutions will not be easy. As an example of that leadership, I am here to proudly introduce to you my running mate and hopefully the next Vice President of the United States, Congressman Robert Hamlin of Illinois," Senator Howard declares in his deep southern accent.

More than 200 members of the media are in attendance at the event. The clicking of cameras can clearly be heard as Hamlin and Howard raise hands above their heads in a very picturesque pose for all to view. Both they and their wives are all smiles, but everyone's happiness is soon challenged by the harsh questions forwarded to them by the media.

"Senator Howard, you spoke of this campaign being about the future and how important an elected official's integrity is. Wanting more responsibility includes acting in a responsible manner. However, you have chosen a running mate half your age that has less than one third your life experiences. How can you, in good conscience, select Representative Hamlin as your running mate?" one reporter asks. As the time progressed, the questions got worse. "Do you not feel that selecting someone who is not yet 30 demeans the office of the vice presidency?" another inquires.

What follows was one of the most polite, but stern responses in political history. "I see where this is going. I understand your hesitance concerning Congressman Hamlin. Believe me, I do. I had many discussions, many heated, about Mr. Hamlin's presence on the ballot. I too questioned whether he was mature and knowledgeable enough for the position. But after many prayers and many talks with others who work and are close to him, the more my doubts became alleviated. The story about his background and what he stands for is truly amazing. Blessed by an incredible amount of luck, he has used his position in U.S. Congress to aid others, not please himself. I myself was surprised. It is a pleasant gift to hear and observe good things about our young people, including Robert Hamlin. I'm rarely humbled in this business, young man, but I could not have made a better decision picking a responsible person as my running mate," Senator Howard announces.

At this time, young Hamlin steps up to the microphone. He begins a slow but confident address to the media.

"I would like to begin by saying I am not a war hero. I have not rescued anyone. And I have indeed been very blessed by God with an extreme sense of good luck in my limited number of years. However, what I do have is the proper knowledge and upbringing to do what is right. There is no need for me to seek forgiveness or sympathy because there are many people in our nation in much worse positions than me," Hamlin says. The tone in his voice is very conversational.

"Allow me the courtesy to explain. I have not done anything wrong, but the direction and intent of your questions appears to indicate an error on someone's part. I understand your doubts. Everyone at one time questions their ability to do certain tasks. I cannot say what has been asked is unfair because life has been very generous to me the past ten years.

"When I was 20 years old I was very fortunate to win the lottery in my home state of Illinois. I shared a pool of $12 million. Since that day, my financial picture has changed dramatically. Although never poor, I am the eldest of five children. My parents worked hard to save and send us to college and teach us to be good people. None of us are in jail and for the most part we turned out okay," Bob says with a smile.

"I soon learned how important money is; everyone wanted it. I chose to give about fifteen percent of what I earn each year, about $50,000, to several different charities. The names of the organizations and how much Tracy and I provide is up here for all of you to review. Previously I've never released this information.

I try to give my time as well, upon request, to various fundraising efforts."

"Also education is very important to me. I give my time trying to change how our public schools are funded. No one can tell me money does not make a difference. It helped me get elected to office and allows me to help others. The fact is that without winning the lottery, nobody would have ever heard of me and, most importantly, the issues I fight for, the same issues I believe in," Bob says with a deep sense of pride. "For me or anyone to say that money has nothing to do with educational or political fortunes would be naive, selfish, and incorrect."

"I completed my studies for my Bachelor and Masters Degrees at Central Illinois University. After one year of law school, I dropped out. It was not because I was doing poorly. In fact, my grades were fine. . . the records of my academic performance are all here for you to review. I just found studying to be boring," Bob says. People in the room began to laugh, after all it was not like dropping out of high school.

"During the spring semester I decided to open my own political consulting firm because I believed it was the best way to help people---by electing people who would use sound judgement in making policy decisions. I have always loved the study of politics. However, I came to appreciate how things could be political in nature without being a candidate. For example, helping someone find a job. Watching them regain their self-respect, pay their taxes, and provide for their children."

"I was approached about running for Congress because the seat was vacant. The incumbent congressman resigned due to poor health. In the race the 'experts' said could not be won - much like our new endeavor we're discussing today - 600 volunteers shocked everyone by helping elect me to the U.S. Congress. I won by 462 votes. People have asked why run? After all, I had everything I needed after winning the lottery. My answer is simple: I have been very blessed and I like helping people. It was my decision to use the money to help make our nation, the wealthiest in the world, a better place to live. Don't misunderstand me. I'm no saint. I like hearing thank you for the time and money I provide. Despite the money, I too am a human being. I felt the best way to give help for the gifts I was blessed with and lucky to be given was to be an active participant in the process. Being there to write legislation and speak about the problems people face to better enable them to pick themselves up."

After briefly pausing, to look as many people as he could in their eyes, Bob continues. I set very hard goals for myself. It is not unusual for me to become swamped with tasks to do. It has not always been easy keeping me on the same page as everyone else. My wife has been very effective at keeping everything in order, to decrease the chance of throwing myself into too many projects. However, I demand a lot of myself. One way to become a better person and achieve great things is by setting difficult goals. . . then working with others to see them realized."

"I enter this race much like I did five years ago in my first campaign: very reluctantly. I did not seek to run with Senator Howard, whom I have always regarded as my political hero. Only after a long phone call did I agree to accept this opportunity. Then I had to speak with my better half to get her consent," Bob says with the media members laughing. "My wife Tracy is a very strong person. Try arguing with her sometime," Bob says.

"Senator Howard is a remarkable human being. It's not just who he is but what he stands for. He has led the fight on many issues. Anyone who is selected for this position has doubts about themselves. To say that I never questioned my level of preparation would be lying. I am not in politics to impose moral or religious rules on anyone. Part of being human is the right to choose: we can do right and help others. . . or we can do wrong and take responsibility for our actions. Many elected officials have become afraid to take unpopular positions, even if it means doing what is right." Bob pauses before continuing his speech. The seriousness in his tone is evident, but not confrontational.

"Over the next few months, you will hear a lot about Senator Howard and me. It's a sad state in our American political system. Hammer your opponent without offering any substantive reasons as to who you are or what you stand for. It is easy to listen to rumors and lies. . . But just take some time to consider the source. For example, are the people making the accusations or 'casting the stone' credible themselves? Are they vocal in their criticism because they stand to gain financially or politically from defeating a proposal made or legislation offered?"

"I want to end by thanking you all for coming today. We will have a lot to discuss in the months ahead and years to come. After all, we all know about my age. However, with the American people's consent and. . . God willing, I modestly accept this new challenge," Bob states to the audience. "I am very proud to have the opportunity to be here today and run with Senator Howard. I came to trust his judgment ten years ago, long before finishing my studies in college. Expecting you all to believe, trust, and respect me would be disrespectful. Many of you are hearing me speak for the first time today. In addition to my age, I hope the future, our economy, and addressing people's needs will also be discussed because they are substantive issues also."

"All I ask is that you give us a chance. There is nothing wrong with being objective. We will take positions that are unpopular. But in the end, the people will know that what we pursue is correct because it will make us all stronger in the future. It will not be hard to recognize the critics. They will be the ones complaining the loudest. In life we learn by listening, not by talking. I express what I feel in my heart to be true. Thank you once again and may God bless you," Bob Hamlin declares to the media. Many people begin to clap, impressed by Bob's candor and sincerity from the speech they just heard. However, some present, just like many of the American citizens, don't believe its Bob Hamlin's or anyone, who has as few birthdays as he does, time.

One month later, long after the Democratic convention had ended and still before the traditional Labor Day kickoff, Robert Hamlin learns what the rest of the nation will soon be told: Senator Howard had just died from a massive heart attack at 12:18 p.m. His shock exceeds that of most people who knew at the time. Earlier it was mentioned that he was only a "heartbeat away" from the presidency if Senator Howard had won. Now the importance of Howard's death hit Bob hard. It is he who is faced with the burden of leading the political campaign against a popular incumbent president forward.

Before the first newscast aired, Robert Hamlin sits down and begins to openly cry.

Chapter Twenty
Losing a Friend Challenges One's Character

Reporters who were present politely excused Bob Hamlin for a few moments. Many had serious doubts about him being the nominee for vice president. However, out of respect for both he and Senator Howard, they turned off the cameras and microphones. It allowed Bob to regain his composure. The shock of Howard's death and the enormous amount of responsibility that comes with running for the presidency was now hitting some reporters. Bob was in Kansas City, Missouri, to address a business luncheon. But at the present moment, all he could think of was the sorrow he felt for Senator Howard's family and how the nation would mourn his absence.

"My heart and support go to the senator's wife and family. It was no secret that he was the one person in politics who I could look to as a teacher. It is not. . . easy to describe how I feel at the present time. It's as if I have lost a member of my own family," Bob declares, his voice growing lower with each word. At this time a reporter speaks up. "Congressman, I know it must be difficult for you, but have you considered the greater implications that Senator Howard's death provides?"

"Thirty minutes ago I learned that Senator Howard had passed away. The only thoughts I have are grief for his family. Our schedules will be adjusted, accordingly, to attend funeral services to mourn the loss of a great person. What was your question in reference to?" Hamlin politely asks.

"It concerns the fact that you would now be the Democratic candidate for president. Under the rules which were changed at your party's convention four years ago, the nominee for vice president moves up and replaces the individual selected as your party's candidate. . . Under the current system, Congressman, YOU now are the presidential nominee."

"I'm truly sorry. My only thoughts the past forty minutes have been of deep sadness for Lillian Howard, her family, and in essence, all of us. At this point in time, who is the nominee is really irrelevant. I have not even considered the issue until you brought it up," Bob replies in a calm and sincere voice. . . "My initial response would be that any comments about that issue would be inappropriate at this time. Maybe everyone involved, including President Crowe and Vice President Marron, could refrain from campaign activities in this time of mourning," Hamlin affirms in a safe but clear tone.

Another reporter then asks, "Are you stating that you have given no thought toward being the nominee? I mean, no thought as to who your running mate would be?"

Bob tries to keep his composure as the reporters' questions become more frequent and more persistent.

"Please bear with me. I really haven't thought about it. Someone who I have deeply respected for a number of years has just passed away. Someone who I believed in, who extended a great deal of trust and responsibility in me, has died. With all due respect, any comments about the election or being president at this time would really be in poor taste," Bob calmly says, his face looking withdrawn from a great deal of sadness he feels.

Five days later, during the announced month of national mourning, Senator Howard's funeral was held in Baton Rouge, Louisiana. A great deal of discussion has been held the previous week as to who would deliver the eulogy for Senator Howard. A public statement offered by Senator Howard's press secretary the day before the funeral soon answered the question. "Mrs. Lillian Howard has asked me to read a brief statement. I will not be taking any questions:

"On behalf of our family, I want to thank the thousands of you who have called, sent letters and shown other expressions of sympathy. Your love and respect have been most appreciated at this difficult time."

"During tomorrow's funeral, the eulogy for my husband will be delivered by Congressman Robert Hamlin, Al's running mate. During the past few months, my husband developed a great deal of respect for the young man from Illinois. . . we have asked him to say a few words at the funeral. We thank you for your kind thoughts this past week. Thank you for keeping us in your prayers. May God bless you all." Sincerely, Lillian Howard.

The funeral was held the following day. "This is a sad day. This scene resembles when Senator Huey Long (from Louisiana) was shot during the Great Depression," one elderly citizen was quoted as saying, with a tear rolling down his eye. We've lost another person from Louisiana who could have become president." The procession of people filing past the body seemed endless. The church was completely full. Admission into the service, attended by most members of the U.S. Congress, President Crowe, and every politician from the state of Louisiana, was granted by invitation only. Approximately 40,000 people gathered outside, listening to the service on loudspeakers. The level of security approached that of a State of the Union address. President Crowe was invited to speak, but respectfully declined to the Howard family beforehand.

The service was held at the same Baptist church where all the Howard family members were baptized, married, and regularly attended church services. After pausing in reflection, Congressman Hamlin rose and walked to the podium. All eyes were fixed on this young person just one month ago was asked to be the running mate of Senator Howard. Thirty days ago, most of America had no idea who this person was. Now he was to speak before a television audience of millions. He took a deep breath before beginning his speech.

"It is with deep honor and sadness that I stand before you today. If it looks that I have difficulty speaking or if my voice suddenly goes, please bear with me. I have a great deal of respect for Senator Howard's family. Because of this, I submitted my notes to Mrs. Howard for review. I've never spoken at a friend's funeral so I am going to do the best I can today.

"On behalf of Mrs. Lillian Howard, I want to thank you for the sympathy and concern thousands of you have shown the past week. We're here today to show our appreciation to the Howard family for the service given to us all by a great person. We may have known Senator Howard for different lengths of time, but anyone who knew him was to love him. Regardless of our political views on the issues that confront us, we all shared a common thread:

Senator Howard was a great human being and we are all better for the contributions he has made. For twenty-four years, he diligently represented the people of Louisiana in Washington D.C. He would have been a great president, perhaps the best our nation has ever known," Congressman Hamlin declares with a firm voice as those in attendance begin to applaud. One by one they slowly rise in respect for Senator Howard's family. For two minutes, the crowd continues in applaud. Their admiration is self-evident.

Bob pauses for about ten seconds. "There is nothing I can say today to ease the pain many of us are feeling right now. One objective we should all have is to pick up the torch that Senator Howard carried during his entire life. We, his supporters, will run as the Democratic presidential nominee in November. Yes, my name will be on the ballot, but as a member of the team, I had planned to work for his various legislative proposals, whether or not he had won this year."

"Timing plays a key part in our lives. Nobody foresaw the events of this past week. There is a time and place for everything. Many people have advised the Howard family and I that maybe we should wait (in his pursuit for the nomination now of the presidency.) When Senator Howard asked me to run, my wife and I wanted to wait.

However, Senator Howard's death has taught us all a valuable lesson. He had been asked, some would say begged, to run in this and the previous two presidential elections. He waited too long and our nation has suffered for it. The proper time to run would be thirty years from now. We were reminded that life is short. We only live once. Senator Howard's death reminds us all that things come to an end. The bottom line is that the issues Senator Howard had spent his entire political career fighting for would also wait 30 years as well."

"Senator Howard was the epitome of honesty and integrity. If I can do one-third in life as Senator Howard performed, then I would have done an admirable job. Sadly, his service to our nation will not be discovered in our history books in the future. However, what is apparent as we gather today is that the principles, his character, and the issues he fought for did create better opportunities and hope for a better future," Bob pronounces as those in the audience all stand and applaud loudly.

"Throughout his career, Senator Howard stated that ours is the greatest country in the history of the world, but that we are not perfect. Being the best is not always good enough. When you are at the top, everyone wants to overtake you. If we are content with just being the best and do nothing to improve ourselves, someday we could be overcome. The problems that we face in our society are the issues that Senator Howard fought and argued that we, as a nation, should address during his career as a public servant. He was always vocal about the need to acknowledge those weaknesses we have. Our nation does not lose on the battlefield or to our competition in the world marketplace. He felt we defeat ourselves when we wait too long to address the problems that confront us," Bob shouted. The audience rose and applauded for more than two minutes.

"We have no problem sending troops overseas. After the mission is accomplished, they return home. Senator Howard deeply felt that the greatest danger we face comes from our own neighborhoods. Many areas look like a war zone. In some schools, we even teach children how to duck when the shooting starts. However, these problems do not end at the city limits. Gang members and other criminals have learned that people in the suburbs have money. They own valuable property and other expensive personal items. Do not think these 'scorns to society' do not care what you own."

"You may be asking why this is important. About six months ago, Senator Howard gave a speech on crime and how life itself seems to have a lower value today. But during his speech, the U.S. Senate chamber was empty. I only know about this because I viewed the speech on cable television. There was no coverage in the newspapers. Senator Howard spoke about how the gangs have been successful at persuading children to become members in their 'clubs of crime.' We as a society do have a stake in what goes on in their neighborhoods. We all pay for the failure to educate our nation's children and teach them respect for each of us as individuals.

"Senator Howard spoke countless times of the importance of education. We as a nation must rise up together to address the issues of school finance and accountability in preparing for the next generation. Our history is full of countless examples of economic success by investing in our young people. Yes, our schools, as does every government body, have waste and levels of inefficiency. Senator Howard worked to provide the necessary resources so all our children can have the money they need, the money they deserve. Senator Howard frequently stated "if we think education is expensive, wait until we learn how much ignorance costs," Hamlin declares to the thunderous applause from those present.

"In many places we can see return on these investments. Wealthier suburbs have pupils with higher test scores. Their parents can afford a quality education. America, Senator Howard argued, was at its best when we invested in ourselves. We need to re-examine what we are doing. If we want to be a nation of retail stores, where higher education is only available for the rich and where the costs of our criminal justice system skyrocket, then we did not heed Senator Howard's warnings."

"Our problems are more complicated than 'us versus them.' If this is how things are going to continue, then Senator Al Howard was wasting his time in the U.S. Senate for eighteen years. Unless we fundamentally alter the path the future holds, then the words of the body lying here before us were in vain. We as a people are better than that, what Senator Howard worked for was better than that, and the condition of the world we leave to our children in the future deserves better than that!" Hamlin affirms to the crowd's approval. Mrs. Howard rises to applaud as many others follow her lead. Despite her grief, she smiles at Bob. She deeply appreciates how Bob recognized Senator Howard's legislative efforts as an elected official, as tears flowed freely down her cheeks.

"I understand how you feel. Believe me I do. I questioned my selection when Senator Howard asked me to be his running mate. I don't know everything. I'm not the most qualified person for this job. But I take solace from knowing that he believed in me and took a chance, at great harm to his political legacy. We can't let him down. I will continue to seek his counsel by prayer and will pursue the passage of policies he fought for in the U.S. Senate. A reason I was asked to run with him was our commitment to his vision for America. From that course, I promise you, we will not sway," Hamlin declares to the audience. The mood of those present is very somber. Accepting Hamlin as the nominee today or next year will not be very easy. Howard's supporters loved him: they just met Robert Hamlin.

"I do not support term limits, but I will offer you one. Today I am declaring that I will seek only one four-year term as the president. If we win, we will not run for reelection four years from now. I intend to dedicate myself to meet our problems as they arise, but lobby for policies to create a better future. After four years as president, regardless of how well the economy is doing or the success of the programs we work for—the same issues Senator Howard had fought for over the past 30 years—we will leave. If the record shows that we lied to you and that we chose to run for reelection, feel free to highlight the broken promise and remove us."

"I had the greatest level of love and respect for Senator Howard. His pursuit for fair play, honesty, improving society, and doing the right thing has been a goal for all of us. His example of hard work and fairness is something I try but have not always succeeded at in my short life. If society and I can try to be one-third the person Senator Howard was, then I know we are doing okay. Please keep him and his family in your prayers and continue to review his numerous position papers and speeches for guidance. Senator Howard's wife, family and the people of Louisiana had the honor of knowing him much longer than we had. The sorrow we all feel from his loss is indeed great. Mrs. Howard, our prayers and thoughts are with you today and in the years to come," Hamlin says to the enthusiastic response of the crowd. Many people are freely crying at this time.

"On behalf of the Howard family, once again thank you for cards, phone calls, and letters of support this past week. It's sad how life works. We never learn how much people loved us until we have left this world. Everyone may not have agreed with him, but they always respected him. His word was better than a signed contract," Hamlin offers. The crowd's response is very enthusiastic, as they rise again in sustained applause.

"He was just that kind of person. After weighing all the facts, he could make a decision and stick with it. I can safely say that his judgment and honor will be greatly missed in America. We need to hold our elected officials accountable to the words, deeds, and efforts as shown by Senator Howard. Call us on the carpet if we betray your trust. You deserve better. After all, you pay our salaries, provide us generous benefits, and place us on our pedestals. If we all could act in the manner established by Senator Howard, we all would be a lot better off. We would each be treated with the respect we deserve because of our status as human beings."

"Mrs. Howard, I close my remarks by thanking you. It would be easy for anyone to misunderstand my speaking today for selfishness, particularly on the content of what has been said. If we have offended anyone today, please accept my apologies. In the limited time we have spent together, Mrs. Howard has extended my wife and me the greatest level of courtesy and friendship. Luckily I have two parents who share the same values exhibited by the Howards. My parents provided me the guidance to learn right from wrong and treat everyone as they would like to be treated. Do I always succeed? No, not at all. But I am constantly reminded by being with people of the character of Senator Al and Mrs. Lillian Howard," Bob says as the audience interrupts his speech by applauding very loudly.

"Allow me to offer one last comment before I sit down and join you for the remainder of this beautiful service. He once stated to me, 'Young Hamlin, you cannot fool everyone in life. When trying, you only make yourself look like the fool. People may not always agree with you. But if you stick to your beliefs, regardless of their popularity, you will be okay. Despite how wealthy you are or how successful you become or how many times you are on television, he told me, don't ever forget who you are, where you came from, the people who inspire you, and what you learned as you were being disciplined by your parents. The paddle hurts when it strikes your behind. But as you go through life, you get hit less frequently and the strikes don't hurt as bad," Hamlin states as many people begin to laugh. Perhaps they each are remembering a conversation they had with Senator Howard during his political career.

Bob turns toward the casket and affirms "Yes Senator Howard, we do hear and we are learning. We have a long way to go. Thank you for your time, your advice, and legislative efforts. May you rest in peace in the presence of God," Hamlin finishes. He departs the

191

podium and joins Mrs. Howard in the pew as the crowd replies with a polite round of standing applause. They exchange a few words and hold each other tightly for a few moments. Across the aisle are seated President Crowe and Vice President Marron, the Republican incumbents in the upcoming fall election. All three exchange greetings. President Crowe whispers something in Hamlin's ear. They both nod to acknowledge what was stated between them. Hamlin then turns around and returns to join his wife for the duration of the service.

Two months pass after Senator Howard's death. On the night before the election, Congressman Hamlin and his running mate, Senator Sam Touter of Georgia, are scheduled to appear in one last televised campaign rally in Los Angeles, California. The speech is set for 7:00 p.m. on the West Coast, 10:00 p.m. Eastern Standard Time. The Hamlin campaign had purchased an hour of time on national television. "Surrogate" speakers were lined up across the nation to credit Bob Hamlin for a great performance. It would allow for the best possible "spin'" afterwards. The rally would be held before 20,000 frenzied supporters of Representative Hamlin and Senator Touter.

Another reason for the excitement was that the "Democratic Duo" as the two were nicknamed by the media, had narrowed the gap significantly. Down at one time by 16 points in their own polling, and as much as 25 points in other independent polls, recent data showed they were now down by two points, well within the infamous "margin of error." Bob Hamlin's campaign had forged a tie with President Crowe in Hamlin's home state of Illinois. Both the state and the election were now within the range for a dramatic upset. As they were introduced the crowd, which had been clapping in unison for twenty minutes, now went wild as the spotlight now shown on them.

As Hamlin approached the microphone, he motioned for the crowd to become quiet. However, such an effort provided worthless as the intensity of their cheering increased. His voice was nearly gone anyway after campaigning sixteen hours a day, each day, for the last two weeks. The event cost $2 million. The crowd's cheering was now causing a delay the staff could not afford. Bob sipped from a glass of water, something he had been doing for the prior six days. He was now trying to force his voice to work one last time in one last act of desperation.

"I truly am sorry. We stand before you tonight strong in spirit, but weak in the voice box. Rest assured tonight's speech will be very short," Bob stated as the crowd booed loudly. They had grown used to his long speeches during this campaign, where the crowd would frequently jump to their feet from the intensity of the emotion he showed in his speeches.

"We haven't slept in two days now. While crossing the nation, meeting new people and giving interviews to members of the media on the plane, my voice has abandoned me so please bear with us. However, regardless of how tired we are, we are energized by your energy and your presence here tonight!" Bob offers as the crowd erupts in applause. "During this race we have made clear that we could not be outworked in this campaign. Our desire is still high and we will continue to push on through tomorrow, Election Day. After all, you'll be out working hard, why should you not expect any less from me?"

"We have two more events scheduled in the next few hours. In Kentucky and Michigan, we have drawn into a near tie with the incumbent president, "Bob stated. He referred to President Crowe as the incumbent, trying to draw upon the mood of not supporting current officeholders across the nation. "Senator Touter and I will be in Lexington, Kentucky at 4:00 a.m. and Detroit, Michigan at 7:00 a.m. Our course has brought us to this point. We have so little time. We cannot afford to sleep because we as a nation cannot afford four more years of the Crowe-Marron Administration!" Hamlin shouts as the crowd jumps to its feet in ecstasy.

"The opposition has stated many things during this race. We all now know that I am 29 years old. We know that I am not a veteran, have no distinguished political record, and did not earn my money the old fashioned way. They are the issues that occupy paid advertisements and public statements made by the incumbents. I brought them up five years ago when I first announced for Congress. But since the race has narrowed and President Crowe has lost what some described as an insurmountable lead, he is now begging for a miracle. He's reaching into his bag of tricks, found nothing there, and is trying to convince you of facts about me that the American people already know."

"Over the past two weeks I have been asked why he is doing it. The answer is actually quite simple: The well of his new ideas, reforms, and leadership has run dry!" Hamlin declares as the crowd roars its approval. "The incumbent president has told you about his successes, what he supposedly has done for you, and what he wants to do if the American people reward him with a second term. Some of us say a second chance," Bob says as the crowd laughs. Thus far, the people have shown their trust in him: his lead has dropped twelve points in the last three weeks and that's in his own (polling) data. We were once written off as dead, down by twenty-five points in the polls, but now the numbers show what those who care about the future already knew: His ship has been hit, the hull is filling up with water, and he is trying to save himself. Thus far, his begging to get a second term at the expense of a nation on auto pilot for previous four years is an insult to the American people," says Hamlin as the crowd applauds wildly.

"You deserve better than that. Since I am only 29, everyone has expected nothing less than that from us. They have demanded honesty and from us they have received it. I have always felt that elected officials should be held to higher standards than most people. After all, the taxpayers provide us with the key to the safe: the right to spend their money. You have the right to ask us difficult questions because you pay our salaries. Contrary to the actions of some, it is not the other way around. You deserve the best, nothing less."

"We do not wish to be viewed as picking on the president. However, the record shows that over the past month, you have heard nothing about education finance, campaign finance reform, a plan for economic development, a vision for the future. . . anything. It's as if the country is on cruise control waiting for something. We know the American people are smarter than that. This race has tightened. My last promise to you is the same as the first one I made at Senator Howard's funeral: we will not run for reelection if you select us tomorrow," Hamlin states. Many boos are heard from the 20,000 people present.

"We understand your concern. However, we will be using our energy to govern. You will not hear about changes we'll propose or the truth second-hand. Having the American people second guess in not leading. We will work with all parties concerned. There will be some needed adjustments in how things are done in creating a better tomorrow. These include some reforms that will allow us to compete in the world marketplace and educate our children so we as a nation can succeed. Remember, nothing comes cheap or free in life. Change will not come without anxiety by the powers that be. If we should go back on our word in four years and even think about running for a second term, then vote us out. If we can't keep our promises like other elected officials who stray from the truth, then keep it for us."

"Thousands of people have generously given of their time in our campaign. Your efforts are greatly appreciated. However, one person is not with us tonight, Senator Al Howard of Louisiana," Hamlin states in a somber voice. The crowd's silence is deafening upon hearing Hamlin's words. "His leadership and his compassion have been noticeably missed for two months now. I miss him terribly. Although his name is not on the ballot, he needs your help tomorrow. His policies, his. . .sincerity is on the line. We need your help."

"We ask that everyone across this great nation come out to vote tomorrow. Some argue that polls or the media decide elections. They don't, the American people do. Whether you support us or not, please exercise your right tomorrow. Doing so serves to better validate the results in the election. The higher the percentage of people who do participate, the more credible the winners are before Congress and the rest of the world."

"Hell, we'd rather you vote for my opponent than not vote at all. . .That way if we lose tomorrow," Bob says as the crowd boos again, we lose knowing that we gave our best shot. That the alternative we offered was not the desired way to go. But if we win...," Hamlin declares as the crowd shouts to indicate they love what they hear. It briefly forces Bob to pause before continuing. "We're going to proceed with the mandate to lead and govern. It can be a mandate to change our lives, change our futures, and change the path for America. We love our nation. As Senator Howard said, we live in

195

the greatest country in the history of the world. However, we can do better. Join us tomorrow—and beyond. Once again, thank you all for all your help and support. May God bless you and your families," Hamlin states.

As he finishes his speech, he bows before the crowd. Senator Touter joins him at the podium. They raise hands as the 20,000 people present give their two nominees a departure and show of support they may never see again. The crowd repeatedly shouts his name, clapping in unison for an additional ten minutes. Hamlin and Touter leave the stage. They still have two more flights and appearances to make in this 24-hour-per-day exhibition known as a presidential campaign.

A commentator for one of the networks states, "Joe, his speech tonight was remarkable. When in the past have you ever heard a politician asking everyone to vote, even those people who have no intention whatsoever to vote for him? From a strategic standpoint, based on the fact that only one of every two people votes, it doesn't make any sense. I do not want to tell people what to do at the polls tomorrow, but I will say this: Congressman Bob Hamlin lacks life experiences from being only 29 years old. Like most Americans, I questioned his qualifications to be the president. I speak with and listen to him, a lot. He has a sincere amount of honesty and candor, rarely seen from our elected officials today. If he were to become president, we'd be in good hands. As a matter of fact. . .maybe he's the breath of fresh air the nation needs," says Mark Askew from the hall.

"Mark, you're a journalist. You can't be making endorsements like that. It weakens our ability to report the news if you're telling people how to vote," Joe Taylor, the senior commentator for the network says.

"I'm prepared to resign tonight from my position if it's asked for. I've been a lifelong member of the other political party. I'm voting for Hamlin tomorrow because. . .I trust him. I've met very few people in life who I truly respect in the world of politics. Understand this: it took a 29-year-old to help me believe in the political system again. That young man's getting my vote tomorrow because he's earned it," Askew replies before the national audience.

Chapter Twenty-One
Let the Future Begin

"It is now 1:20 a.m. I have just been told that Congressman Hamlin spoke with President Crowe about ten minutes ago. The president expressed his congratulations to Congressman Hamlin. I repeat, as you have just heard, our network has just declared Congressman Robert Hamlin the winner in Kentucky, Michigan, and Georgia. Regardless of who wins Pennsylvania, regardless of who wins the popular vote - which may not be decided until tomorrow - Congressman Robert Hamlin has just been elected the 46th President of the United States," says Charles Rose, a long-term political correspondent.

"Charlie, are you sure? I mean, the other networks have not yet awarded the election to Hamlin," inquires Tom Johnson the lead political commentator.

"Yes, I was just told that Robert Hamlin will address the nation in fifteen minutes. He will speak before this. . . throng of supporters here in Chicago."

"How can he?" states Johnson.

"I'm not sure. But I can say that reliable sources with whom I have spoken with told me that President Crowe did call to concede, to admit defeat, just moments ago. The vote totals are VERY close, some states are still too close to call. But President Crowe called to say that he does feel that he has indeed lost. For whatever reason, he has chosen to give his concession speech in a few minutes," Charlie Rose replies.

About thirty-five minutes later, after President Crowe graciously acknowledged defeat to his supporters, the tension rises. The Hamlin supporters are ecstatic with the rumor that Congressman Hamlin will come down to address them shortly. Nearly 3,000 people are still crammed into the downtown Chicago hotel (with police estimates of another 20,000 gathered in the streets outside) as the time is approaching 1:45 a.m. Five minutes later a large group of Secret Service agents, political leaders, and the families of Congressman Hamlin and Senator Touter begin to gather on the stage. Hamlin and

Touter are waiting behind the main stage, where the crowd cannot see them. Governor Jim Mears of Illinois, a friend of Hamlin, speaks to the crowd.

"Within the past hour, we received a phone call from President Crowe. He and Congressman Hamlin had a friendly and polite discussion about the campaign that concluded today. As you well know, it has indeed been a LONG day. So without any further delay, I am very proud to have the great honor to introduce to you, the next President of the United States, Robert A. Hamlin," Governor Mears shouts as the crowd becomes delirious with the excitement of winning a presidential election. After a brief walk through the families and political friends present, all restrained by the Secret Service officials on hand, Hamlin and Touter arrive on the stage.

Now on the stage, they are clearly visible to all in the crowd. The sound level reaching upward hits so hard it has the effect of "denting the roof." With each movement around the stage by the winners, the noise grows. Hamlin is clearly moved emotionally by the response from the crowd. He wants to speak, but the crowd will not let him. As they begin chanting "HAM-LIN, HAM-LIN, HAM-LIN," Bob begins to break down. The lack of sleep recently, combined with the emotion from the campaign during the previous three months, now hit him. He tries to cover his face so people do not see the tears rolling down his cheeks.

As the crowd continues to clap and chant his name, Hamlin approaches the podium again. The noise soon lowers after Bob begins to speak.

"I must apologize once again. My voice is shot, I have not slept in two days, but BOY do I feel good!!" Hamlin declares as the crowd's cheering is comparable to that of a volcano's eruption. "I received a phone call from President Crowe a short time ago. He was very kind and polite. He stated that it was his belief that he had indeed lost and wanted to concede," Bob states as the crowd cheers wildly. The cheer sounded like a train's horn ringing while passing a station. For two minutes the noise grows.

Bob resumed his speech. "I have many people to thank. My family, my friends, and my wife. . . my office and campaign staff, the list could go on forever. From those of you who helped elect me as a congressman, to those of you across the nation. Your help, your trust in me, your faith is very humbling. The best way to show our gratitude is to demonstrate through our actions and live up to the promises we made. One cannot fully appreciate the level of trust you have granted us. For those of you who did not vote for us, we respect your opinions. We won't agree on each issue, but we will try to earn your faith by working hard and keeping our word. I intend to keep every vow I made.

And that includes the following: We will not run for reelection . . . My wife will be glad that my political career will be ending soon, that there is a light at the end of the tunnel. As she sees it, will end in four years," Bob states as the crowd laughs.

"Senator Touter and I will do our utmost to do what is right. We don't have an easy job ahead of us. Many times in my short life I have been told to slow down. . . take a step back. You know, when I was younger than I am now," Hamlin states as he pauses. The crowd is laughing as he continues with a smile on his face. . . "I was once given the nickname *The Epitome of Motivation.* My peers felt I was always doing something. . . oftentimes more than one task at once. . . not always doing any one task at hand well," Bob says. Those still present are laughing. "Always going, just like that bunny. However, if we are not successful these next four years, it will not be because we didn't try," Hamlin says.

"Besides my wife and Senator Touter and my parents, there is one last person who is not with us tonight who we must mention. I know it's hard to remain quiet, but if we can have your attention for a brief moment, it would mean a great deal. . .Thanks. Four months ago I was asked by Senator Al Howard to be his running mate. For many reasons, some that we may never know, he offered me the chance to run with him. Since that day, and in particular the day he passed away, I've tried my best to show that I am worthy of the trust that Senator Howard saw in me. To this day, I still seek his guidance and advice through prayer. He may not be with us, but he will always be speaking from the policies we push for and the causes we pursue. We will push for legislative approval for the issues that Senator Howard pursued during the 24 years he represented Louisiana, whose state voted for us today. Because of this, Senator

Touter, Senator Howard and I won tonight," Hamlin declared as the crowd roars its approval. "More importantly, you won."

"Tonight the American people have judged us ready to lead. At a minimum, they deserve from us a full faith effort and the integrity to pursue our objectives. After all, they pay the bills. You work hard and pay the taxes to provide the money for the services government offer. We will do the best we can to give you a nation and a government you can be proud of."

"One final message we want to convey is to all the young people in America tonight. I hope you're not up because tomorrow is a school day," Hamlin says drawing laughter from the crowd. "But if there is any part of my speech I would like for the media to carry is the next few days is the following: The problems facing the inner cities and our young people are indeed serious. From peer pressure to drugs to violence and to life in the fast lane, there are many choices available to keep you from the right path. These problems are part of the reason I first got into politics, despite hating it when I was in high school. Many people told me I was too young for this or that, much like what young Americans hear on a daily basis. But in the end, if you work hard in school, honor your parents, show respect for your peers, and do the best you can, things will work out and take care of themselves," Hamlin states to a cheering audience.

"Young Americans, stand proud. Your lives do have value. Your lives, as human beings as well as the lives of your neighbors, are important. We must learn to get along with one another. Violence does not solve anything, contrary to what you see in certain movies. The sooner we'll learn to place value on our own lives, the sooner we'll be able to live and work with each other. You are the dreamers. With your help, we can accomplish great things."

"We cannot build today's houses with tomorrow's bricks. Starting tomorrow, we will begin the long journey that awaits us. We hope and pray that America can begin a course for a better future. Thanks again. May God bless you all," Hamlin states when concluding his speech. Senator Touter and he raise their arms at the front of the stage, smiling as they wave to the cheering crowd. After being joined by their wives, they leave the stage and are escorted to their private rooms.

"Politics. . . campaigns. . .The Presidency," Robert Hamlin mumbles to himself. "Unbelievable."

It is now 8:53 a.m. Robert Hamlin awakes from his sleep for the final time from a dream that began the previous evening. The last four hours uninterrupted by his sweat or other disturbances in the house. After going to the bathroom, Bob goes downstairs to the kitchen where his parents join him. They are reading the newspaper and eating breakfast. His father asks if he would like some coffee, but he respectfully declines. "No, I'm sorry Dad, but I cannot stand the stuff. It tastes horrible. Besides, that's the devil's brew," Bob jokingly replies with a smile.

After some casual talk, Bob brings up the topic from the day before: his future.

"Mom, you may not believe this, but I did a lot of thinking last night about a career," Bob offers.

'Wow. That's great. Any new leads on what you'd like to do?" Mrs. Hamlin asks.

"Yea. I think I want to study politics," he replies as his father spits out the coffee from his mouth. What food or drink did not leave his mouth he begins to cough and choke on.

"Are you okay?" Bob slowly asks, after waiting for his father to finish coughing.

"Yeaaa. . . I'm okay," Mr. Hamlin answers while removing the napkin from his mouth. His father whispers in a very low voice, "I'm fine. Are you trying to kill me? Politics? Give me a break!!!"

"Well. . . That's an interesting choice," Mrs. Hamlin states while looking at her husband with a confused look on her face.

"I must admit it's something I don't think much about. . . Then again I have not considered too many fields, but I think it's something I could handle. There are some people on my floor who are taking those classes. Perhaps they could give me some more information," Bob states.

The three of them continue talking a few more minutes about school and Bob's weekend at home.

"Well, before I return to school today I need to clean my room. If I have extra time, maybe I'll vacuum the car for you," Bob says. His parents planned to drop him off at the mall near Joliet, Illinois where the buses met to pick up students returning to Central Illinois University.

"I really need to write down some ideas on how to improve myself for this. I mean, I have no idea about giving or. . . even writing a speech. I'll be upstairs," Bob says as he departs the room. He continues to mumble to himself (a common habit) as he walks away.

After he leaves, Mr. Hamlin drops his cup of coffee and it breaks on the floor. He does not move to clean it up because he is staring out the room, watching Bob go up the stairs. "Political Science?" Mr. Hamlin questions. "Two years of college and our son has learned nothing," Mr. Hamlin declares. "How much did we spend?"

"That's my son!!" Mrs. Hamlin shouts, slapping her hands together. "Somehow I knew he could make a decision. Deep within that layer of stubbornness lays a very motivated person. HEY BOB! WHAT MADE YOU CHOOSE THAT FIELD?" Mrs. Hamlin yells toward Bob, who by now was in his bedroom.

Bob slams the door behind him and looks into the mirror. To answer his mother's concerns he calmly states, "Sometimes we may not know the answers to the important questions in our lives. That is why it is often revealed to us. What we do with it after we see our destiny is then up to us as individuals. It's time to turn the page. . . Let the future begin," Bob whispers with a large smile on his face and fist raised into the air - to anyone who would listen.

THE END